TOO HEAVY FOR YOUR POCKET

BY JIRÉH BREON HOLDER

★

★

DRAMATISTS
PLAY SERVICE
INC.

for my mother,
Cassandra Holder Christiansen,
a well of love, patience, & gratitude

with my deepest gratitude to each of the Freedom Riders
for their sacrifice.

The world premiere of TOO HEAVY FOR YOUR POCKET was produced by the Alliance Theatre (Susan V. Booth, Artistic Director) in Atlanta, Georgia, in February 2017. It was directed by Margot Bordelon, the scenic design was by Reid Thompson, the lighting design was by Liz Lee, the costume design was by Sydney Roberts, and the sound design was by Elisheba Ittoop. The cast was as follows:

BOWZIE	Stephen Ruffin
SALLY	Markita Prescott
TONY	Rob Demery
EVELYN	Eboni Flowers

The New York City premiere of TOO HEAVY FOR YOUR POCKET was produced by Roundabout Theatre Company as part of Roundabout Underground at the Harold and Miriam Steinberg Center for Theatre on October 5, 2017. It was directed by Margot Bordelon, the scenic design was by Reid Thompson, the costume design was by Valérie Thérèse Bart, the lighting design was by Jiyoun Chang, the sound design was by Ian Scot, the hair and wig design was by Dave Bova and J. Jared Janas, the production stage manager was Katherine Wallace, and the assistant stage manager was Sara Sahin. The cast was as follows:

BOWZIE	Brandon Gill
SALLY	Nneka Okafor
TONY	Hampton Fluker
EVELYN	Eboni Flowers

ACKNOWLEDGMENTS

If a play is lucky it can have a long life which has been touched by the actors who inhabited its characters throughout its development. I offer my boundless gratitude to:

Britny Horton (my sister), Freddie Fulton (my brother), Shaunette Renee, Chalia Ayers LaTour (my tribe), Jonathan Majors, Condola Rashad, Jeremy Pope, Joshua Boone, Maechi Aharanwa, Danielle Brooks, Jeremie Harris, John Stewart III, Shannon Dorsey, Justin Weaks, Kashayna Johnson, Sheria Irving,

the formidable cast of the Alliance Theatre production: Stephen Ruffin, Nicolette Robinson, Markita Prescott, Rob Demery,

as well as the astounding cast of the Roundabout Theatre Company production: Brandon Gill, Eboni Flowers, Nneka Okafor, and Hampton Fluker.

CHARACTERS

BOWZIE BRANDON, a trip

SALLY-MAE CARTER, fine even though she's expecting

TONY CARTER, a hard man with a soft smile

EVELYN BRANDON, a singer

*These characters are of African-American descent
& each production of this play should reflect that*

PLACE

Nashville, Tennessee

TIME

Summer of 1961

SPACE

Grass everywhere, even indoors

NOTE ON MUSIC

Permission to perform the song sung by Evelyn on page 62, written by Ian Scot and Jiréh Breon Holder, is included with a performance license for the play. No performance rights to any other song is included in such license.

For information regarding all other music mentioned in the play, including but not limited to songs noted by an asterisk (*), please see Note on Songs/Recordings on page 88.

TOO HEAVY FOR YOUR POCKET

ACT ONE

1

Lights up slowly on Bowzie Brandon, a twenty-year-old, scrawny kind of man. He is in the middle of an open field looking to the sky.

His toes sink into the earth.

He takes the time to feel the breeze.

He lets his feet sink into the soft, damp earth. The grass slides between his toes.

He is a tree.

He breathes hard; a half-prayer, half-declaration: Huh!

And again. Huh!

And again. Huh!

He smiles.

Then laughs heartily.

A room is revealed that might be a dining room, living room, or kitchen depending on the arrangement of the furniture. It almost reminds you of the house your grandparents might have lived in except there is no floor. Just beautiful green grass in the place of creaky wooden boards.

There is a handmade table with four handmade chairs. The kitchen supplies are all third- or fourth-hand. The quarters are cozy enough for the audience to feel like guests.

Sally enters. She is so slight one might not realize she is pregnant. She reminds you of your daughter or your younger sister, or possibly a photo of your mother when she was a teenager.

She sings a bit, pulling out a commencement cap and gown.

She grins a little as she hangs it up. The gorgeous regalia is beckoning her, so she tries on the cap. She thinks about trying on the gown. She almost decides, "To heck with it—Why not!" When Bowzie enters the home.

BOWZIE. Hey now Sally, Looking mighty sharp.
Don't hurt 'em!

SALLY. *(Embarrassed.)* Don't be sneaking up on me like that!
What's wrong with you?

BOWZIE. I ain't seen you smile like that since the day Tony proposed.
You about to be a educated Negro, for sure!

SALLY. Bowzie[1], what are you doing here?

BOWZIE. I woke up at the crack of dawn to make it *all* the way to Haynes.

SALLY. The school needs tutors on a Saturday?

BOWZIE. So they said.
When I got there, there wasn't a single soul there.
You try to help niggahs out, and this is what you get.

1 Pronounced "Boe-zee"

SALLY. You know I don't take no ugly words, Bowzie Brandon.

BOWZIE. You know I'm right.

SALLY. Don't mean you got to be nasty about it.
Though, you think they'd be wiser than that.

BOWZIE. How you figure?

SALLY. Wasting the time of a future Fisk University student!

BOWZIE. Here you go.

SALLY. I'm sorry, I'm sorry.

BOWZIE. I ain't a student yet.
I'm just another raggedy brother begging for a handout.

SALLY. Hush.

BOWZIE. Until I have a degree in my hand, you the biggest some-
body around these parts.
Miss Sally-Mae Carter!
Beautician Extraordinaire!
Certified by Joyce Howard School of Glamour—

SALLY. *(Cutting to the chase.)* You haven't heard *any* word yet?
They said you should have gotten a letter by now.

BOWZIE. You as bad as Evelyn[2].
Every evening she come home just running for the mailbox.
I say, "Baby, is you married to the mailbox or to me?"

SALLY. And what she say?

BOWZIE. She tell me she's mine for sure,
but the mailbox is putting up a good fight for her attention.

SALLY. *(Laughing.)* She ain't got no sense!

> *Tony, Sally's husband, enters rubbing the sleep from his eyes.*
> *He is Bowzie's bosom buddy since childhood, twice his size*
> *and all muscle. It's not hard to tell that Bowzie is the brains*
> *and Tony is the brawn.*

TONY. Bowzie, you here already?
Why you ain't wake me up?

BOWZIE. What you think I'm here for?

---

2 Pronounced "Ev'lyn"

SALLY. What are you two up to?

TONY. Man business, woman.

What you doing up?

You supposed to be resting for your big day.

SALLY. Why? So both of us can be sleeping in?

I'm going to the outhouse.

Y'all try to stay out of trouble.

>*Sally exits out of the house.*

>*The men wait until she's gone to snap into action:*

>*Tony rushes to a corner of his things and pulls out a hidden bundle of dollar bills.*

TONY. I thought you wasn't gonna be able to come 'til right before graduation.

BOWZIE. I made it all the way to Haynes and wasn't nobody there

TONY. Niggahs don't appreciate nothing.

Go'n ahead and pick it up.

Just honk when you get back.

BOWZIE. Sally gon' hop clear out her skin.

TONY. Here's the rest of the money I owe them.

>*Tony holds out a few dollar bills from the stash.*

BOWZIE. Naw, it's Sally's big day.

This one's on me.

>*Bowzie shows Tony money from his own pocket.*

TONY. You sure y'all can afford it?—

BOWZIE. Don't mention it.

TONY. Thank you, brother.

BOWZIE. Be back in a shake!

>*Bowzie exits.*

>*Tony quickly replaces his hidden stash of dollar bills.*

>*Sally enters.*

SALLY. Where Bowzie go?

TONY. That ain't none of my business.

SALLY. What you talking?

TONY. I ain't doing no talking.
Not when there's so much to *look* at.

SALLY. I don't know what you looking at.

TONY. This foxy young thang right before my eyes.

SALLY. Charm the stripes off a tiger.

TONY. *Mm mm mm.*
Finer than frog's hair.
How you gets to be that fine, girl?

SALLY. Let me be, man.
I need to get dressed.

TONY. Naw naw naw.
I ain't letting you get dressed yet.

> *Tony advances, and a giggling Sally runs into the back room.*
>
> *Tony follows her, hands poised for her backside.*
>
> *A brief beat passes before Sally reenters with her dress and heels.*

SALLY. Let me get dressed.

> *Tony reenters, still playfully chasing her.*

TONY. You ain't listening.
I'm trying to get you *undressed.*

> *Sally puts her hands on her hips.*

SALLY. Tony Carter.

> *Tony knows what this means. He acquiesces.*

TONY. At least let me lend you a hand, baby.

> *Tony helps Sally with her dress, spending special time with her belly. Sally nervously accepts the gentle gesture. It's almost romantic, but something lurks underneath. Both spouses stop themselves just short of surrendering to the intimacy.*
>
> *Interrupting the beat, Evelyn, Bowzie's wife, enters singing as she often does. A gospel song, such as something by Rev. Robert Ballinger.* She is a beautiful chocolate woman with a full figure.*

EVELYN. Morning, y'all.

TONY and SALLY. Morning, Evelyn.

EVELYN. *(Spotting the gown.)* Ooh, wee!

Let's put it on!

> *Evelyn helps Sally finish dressing, all the while singing. Tony might join in adorning Sally for her day.*

Happy graduation!

SALLY. Thank you, girl.

> *A loud car honk from outside.*

What was that?

EVELYN. Beats me.

One of your country neighbors come into money?

SALLY. Not that I know of.

> *This time a loud, long honk.*

EVELYN. Well, I know what! Whoever it is ain't gon' keep up that noise.

> *Evelyn goes to the door and opens it.*

Well, I'll be.

Get on over here, Sally-girl.

SALLY. What?

EVELYN. Just get on.

> *Sally goes to the door and sees the shiny car.*

SALLY. Get on out of town.

EVELYN. Fresh coat of paint and all.

TONY. Aw, woman. Can't have you walking to your own graduation.

> *Bowzie enters, grinning.*

BOWZIE. Was she surprised?

TONY. As all get-out!

SALLY. You got the car back?

I thought the repossession man took it two weeks ago?

BOWZIE. You know Tony love a surprise.

He only told you that so he could take it to the paint shop.

SALLY. Well let's get going!

TONY. Where we gots to go?

Graduation don't start for another hour.

SALLY. I need to stop by Otis at the Bi-Rite.

TONY. Woman, write down a list for Bowzie to read
and *we'll* run get it. Today *your* day.
My Queen of Sheba ain't lifting a finger.

EVELYN. Quit lying.
Knowing y'all just wanna show off that Chevy—

BOWZIE. *(With some grandeur.)* Pretty Green Chevy.

EVELYN. What?

BOWZIE. Gots to say it like that now: *Pretty Green Chevy.*

EVELYN. *(Ignoring him.)* Just wanna make sure the neighborhood
get a good look.

BOWZIE. Sally, you should've known
your mister wasn't gon' let you walk to your own graduation.

SALLY. Fault me for thinking he had any sense.
(To Tony.) You said you was out working when you come home late
this week,
but you was gambling.

TONY. Bowzie, was I working?
Since she don't never believe me.

BOWZIE. I'm a witness.
He been planning it for days.
(Imitating Tony.) "Come hell or high water, that car is gonna be
decked out for Sally's day."

SALLY. *(Handing him a list.)* Bowzie, can you read my writing?

BOWZIE. Right fine penmanship it is, Sally.

EVELYN. And come back directly.

BOWZIE. Yes, baby.

TONY. Bye now.

SALLY. Hurry back.

> Bowzie and Tony exit.
> The sound of the Chevy driving off.

I should've known.

EVELYN. How you supposed to know?

SALLY. Tony got a pregnant woman at home and out gambling.

EVELYN. That's better than what you thought he was doing.

SALLY. All I need is him to bring his behind *home*.

EVELYN. Sally, you not thinking straight.
How you gon' walk all the way to Jefferson Street?
God only knows how you been making it this whole time for your classes.

SALLY. On a bus and a prayer like I get everywhere.
I was glad to see that Chevy go.

EVELYN. Girl, you got to let him be a man. That's all.

SALLY. I'm fine with him being a man.
It's him being a fool that I can't take too much more of.

EVELYN. You act like I ain't married to a fool, too.

SALLY. At least your fool stay in line.

EVELYN. That's 'cause Bowzie come home to a mean wife.

     They laugh.

SALLY. Well, I wanna be mean.

EVELYN. Mean as a snake like me?

SALLY. Meaner.

EVELYN. Well first you gotta fix your face.
Can't be walking around grinning all the time like you do.

SALLY. How I gotta look?

EVELYN. Like somebody just spat on your shoe.

SALLY. *(Demonstrating.)* Like this?

EVELYN. You look like you 'bout to go in labor, girl.
No. *(Demonstrating.)* Like this.

SALLY. Okay, okay. I got it now.

EVELYN. Put your eyebrows into it and puff your cheeks a little!

     More laughter, then a beat.

SALLY. So how you faring?

     Evelyn tries to ignore her, but Sally gives her a knowing look.

EVELYN. You know me. Take a world of trouble to bend me out of the right shape.

SALLY. Ain't no shame in being sad.
It's been a year.

EVELYN. God needed another angel. My baby is safe in God's hands. Ain't nothing to be sad about.

SALLY. You sure?

EVELYN. I'm sure, girl. Now, let me be.
You know I don't do good with feelings and all. I'm a stone-cold fox.

SALLY. Sho' is.

EVELYN. Happy birthday to my baby angel.

SALLY. Happy birthday to your baby angel.

EVELYN. *(Shifting.)* And her godsister will be here soon enough.

SALLY. Shoot, the sooner the better.

EVELYN. *(To Sally's stomach.)* You just take your time, little princess.

SALLY. Already a bad influence, Auntie Evelyn.

    A honk.

EVELYN. Let's go show them what's what!

    Laughter as the women exit.

3

Bowzie in the field again.
He fiddles with a letter in his hands. Thinks real hard about whether to open it or tear it to pieces.
He opens it.
He reads it slowly.
Couldn't be. He reads it over.
And over.
He walks away reading it again.

Sally is in the final stages of preparing supper when Bowzie enters with his shirt in his hands.

BOWZIE. Knock knock?

SALLY. You steady showing up to folk house early.

BOWZIE. Just figured I'd take a little stroll.

SALLY. Half-naked?

BOWZIE. It's nice day out!

SALLY. Feel like the sun's fit to explode to me.

BOWZIE. I like it hot.
Make you feel alive.
Like you can feel the blood running through your veins.

SALLY. I reckon that means you don't want no ice water or cold drink[3]?

> *Bowzie goes to the fridge.*

BOWZIE. Don't get ahead of yourself, now.
Say, what you cooking?

SALLY. Get from my kitchen, boy.
If you want to help, you can set the table.

BOWZIE. Just you, me, Tony, Evelyn?

SALLY. Who else would be coming?
Between your little celebration last week and my graduation party week before,
I'd be fine if I didn't see nobody else 'til Christmas.

BOWZIE. Sure[4] 'nough!

> *They move in silence for a moment. The sound of food cooking and tableware being set.*

Hey, Sally.
You think Evelyn proud of me?

3 Any carbonated beverage

4 Pronounced "shol"

SALLY. Proud of you?
What kind of question is that.

BOWZIE. Just a question.

SALLY. 'Course she proud of you.
Made sure your whole family came from Dry Creek to celebrate your acceptance letter.
And you know that gang don't leave they house for much.

BOWZIE. Trifling. You can say it.

SALLY. I ain't gon' speak ill of nobody, but a few choice words do come to mind.

BOWZIE. Tri-ful-ling!

SALLY. Well!

BOWZIE. Naw, I mean do you think she *proud* though?

SALLY. Where's this coming from? She say something?
You know Evelyn just be talking.

BOWZIE. I'm just saying.
You think she'd be more proud if I did something else?
What if I signed up to be an astronaut?
Be the first man on Mars?

SALLY. Man on Mars?
Bowzie Brandon,
I can't think of nothing on God's earth
that could possibly make Evelyn more proud
than you being the first man in this whole neighborhood to go to college.

BOWZIE. Shucks, I guess you right.

>   *Tony enters.*

TONY. How you gon' be early to dinner, Negro?

SALLY. Distracting me from cooking.

TONY. Hey, baby.

>   *Sally and Tony kiss.*

SALLY. Glad you made it home at a decent hour tonight.

TONY. *(Diverting.)* Don't you know that's rude, man.

BOWZIE. What's rude?

TONY. Company showing up to folk' house early.

BOWZIE. So I'm "company" now?

SALLY. Let him alone.

TONY. Family or company, you here. Let's play some cards.

> *They start playing cards.*
>
> *Evelyn enters.*

EVELYN. I ain't miss nothing did I?

SALLY. Not a thing.

BOWZIE. Apparently, I'm rude.

TONY. Could take a cue from your wife here and arrive at folk house at a Godly hour.

SALLY. If y'all don't hush up.
Evelyn, come taste this.

EVELYN. Girl, let me get a drink first.
I already run a little hot.
The sun's trying to explode out there.

> *Evelyn grabs a cold drink from the fridge.*

SALLY. Bowzie say when the temperature get higher than ninety degrees, you supposed to start stripping.

BOWZIE. Oh Lord.

EVELYN. Bowzie, put your clothes on.
You think this was your house the way you carry on.

TONY. I tried to tell him.

BOWZIE. You ain't nothing.

EVELYN. Oh, Sally-girl. I swung by Giant Foods to grab some snap beans and tomatoes—

SALLY. You grab me some?

EVELYN. You know I did.
Anyway, they was going on and on about your graduation.
You got all Davidson County talking about it.

TONY. That ceremony was something else, wasn't it?

SALLY. Well, it was something alright.

TONY. Something out of sight.

SALLY. If you don't quit.
That was over a week ago—

BOWZIE. Folks still talking about how they stopped traffic on Jefferson Street.
Jefferson Street!
For a whole mess of Negro women in their cap and gowns
headed to the big old Howard Church!
I thought pigs was gonna be flying.

TONY. I tell you who was the *foxiest* lady in the number.

BOWZIE. Who?
'Cause I bet money it was that Martha Scruggs. *Whew boy!*

TONY. Martha Scruggs couldn't hold a candle to this one. Let me tell it.

SALLY. Go'n now.

TONY. Men lining up here to yonder
to see this young thing rolling out of a *Pretty Green Chevy.*
Would say it's Eartha Kitt
exceptin' she got *hips*!

SALLY. Evelyn, I sure wish these men would hush already.

BOWZIE. Uh oh.

EVELYN. *(To Bowzie.)* Why ain't you put your shirt on like I told you?

SALLY. Bowzie been bare-chest since we was little.
I'm just happy he got on britches.

BOWZIE. You call these britches? I been meaning to ask you to sew me some more.

EVELYN. So now you too good for britches?

TONY. He a big college boy. What'd the letter say, again?

SALLY. Say "Fisk University would be honored to accept you on a full academic scholarship."

BOWZIE. "*Pending* the completion of remedial summer courses."

EVELYN. You skipped the part where they talk about his "distinguished accomplishments."

SALLY. How could I forget?

TONY. Bowzie, tell us again what kind of *distinguished accomplishments* you been making.

SALLY. The kind that get you a *full academic scholarship.*

BOWZIE. For tuition. That's all it cover.
They making me do summer school, ain't no full scholarship for that.

TONY. You got to pay for two months of school and get four years free, man.

BOWZIE. Let's talk about Sally some more.

TONY. Well all I know is a big college boy with *distinguished accomplishments*
can't be wearing no raggedy britches.

SALLY. Raggedy, I hear?

EVELYN. They wasn't raggedy last week.

TONY. Well I reckon he wasn't no college boy last week!

SALLY. Well, you done gone off and ruined the surprise…

BOWZIE. Sure 'nough?

SALLY. Should we?

TONY. Dinner can wait!

EVELYN. I told them they going too far—

SALLY. Too far nothing. How's this for britches?

    Sally reveals a freshly made suit.

BOWZIE. Boy, these are sharp!

TONY. Ain't nothing without a good jacket though!

BOWZIE. Brother!

SALLY. Here you go!

BOWZIE. Y'all 'bout to make me cry.

TONY. Sally made it soon as you applied.

SALLY. I just knew you was gonna get in.

TONY. First, Sally graduate glamour school; now you going to college. Two grade-A Einsteins.

BOWZIE. Y'all too much.

SALLY. We so proud of you we don't know what to do with ourselves.

EVELYN. Look at him. All blubbery.

SALLY. Well, try it on!
Go'n use the back room.

TONY. Acting like you ain't never seen a suit before.

>   *Bowzie exits to the back room to change.*

SALLY. *(To Tony.)* He's come a long way from when you tried to squeeze in his Sunday suit for our first date.

TONY. Bowzie wasn't right.
He knew I looked like stuffed turkey!

EVELYN. Ooh, I just love this story.

TONY. That was the minute that man became my brother.
I couldn't read; couldn't write; didn't have but two pair of drawers to my name.
But he lent me that suit so I could look like something when I courted her.
I still can't believe Sally let me hold her hand on that hayride.

SALLY. Like you would've took "no" for an answer.

EVELYN. And then, Sally said…

TONY. What'd you say, baby?

SALLY. Told him, he can hold my hand all he wants.
But I can't entertain nobody who don't come to church with me and meet my daddy.

TONY. That put the fear of God in me.
I had heard stories about Saddidy[5] Sally-Mae.

SALLY. Get on.

BOWZIE. *(Calling.)* Baby, bring me my shoes!

TONY. I knew if was going with her to church I had to come *correct*.
Ain't that right, baby?
Her daddy didn't play.

SALLY. Still don't.

EVELYN. So Bowzie let you borrow his Sunday suit.
Even taught you the Sunday hymnal so you could sing along with Sally.

5 Snooty or uppity

SALLY. *(Wistfully.)* Those were the days…

> *Sally reveals a cake.*

EVELYN. My, my, my.

TONY. *(Whispering.)* I say we go'n 'head and surprise him with it.

SALLY. Before dinner?

BOWZIE. I'm coming out!

> *Sally quickly hides the cake.*
>
> *Bowzie enters, looking like a million-dollar bill.*

Well…

How I look?

EVELYN. Sally outdid herself with this, baby.

SALLY. Don't even look like Bowzie no more!

TONY. That's what a college boy supposed to look like!

EVELYN. Still got those skinny little chicken legs though.

> *Sally reveals the cake.*

BOWZIE. This ain't what I think it is.

SALLY. Mama Nola's famous strawberry cake.

EVELYN. Your favorite.

TONY. Hip hip!

SALLY and EVELYN. Horray!

TONY. Hip hip!

SALLY and EVELYN. Horray!

TONY. Hip hip!

SALLY and EVELYN. Horray!

> *Bowzie fights back tears.*

EVELYN. Well, say something, man. We went through all that.

TONY. I think I need to hear a speech. You know Bowzie speechify better than Dr. King.

EVELYN. Whole county know Bowzie can give a good old speech.

SALLY. Alright now, let the man talk.

> *Several moments of silence.*
>
> *Bowzie hesitates.*

Then smears his hand in the cake, before exiting hastily.

EVELYN. What the hell?

SALLY. Maybe he just needed to use the outhouse.

TONY. Are you crazy, man?!

EVELYN. Ain't nobody got to pee that bad.

TONY. He crazy!

SALLY. Y'all want a piece?

EVELYN. I know you done seen what just happened!

SALLY. He just got some butterflies is all.

TONY. Butterflies hell. I'm fixing to show him some butterflies.

Tony exits.

EVELYN. Aw hell.
I should've known when they ain't fight at your graduation,
we ain't have much longer 'til a ruckus break loose.

SALLY. You know those two can't get along *with* each other, can't
get along without.
Cake?

EVELYN. You too calm for me, Sally-Mae.

SALLY. What use getting riled up?
They gon' be just fine come sun-up.
You sure you don't want a piece?
Don't let my big tail be the only one eating.

EVELYN. You ain't big, girl. You *full*.

SALLY. *(Presenting her belly.)* You ain't nothing but a tale. I'm big
as a house.

EVELYN. *(Sing-song.) But you quiet as a church mouse.*

SALLY. *(Distracting her.)* Mmm. You know we love to hear you sing.
Sing some more, Auntie Evelyn.

Evelyn does. Something sweet like the Drifters or the Spinners.*

Mmm.
The voice of an angel.

EVELYN. It's real nice what you done for my Bowzie.

SALLY. Me and Tony so proud we could burst.

23

EVELYN. That's what I'm scared he gon' do.

SALLY. Just butterflies. That's all.

EVELYN. Sure 'nough?

SALLY. Sure 'nough.

5

Bowzie stands center.
Tony enters.

TONY. You got a lot of nerve, partner.
Your scrawny ass better get back in there and eat that cake
or we gon' have to dance.

BOWZIE. College.

TONY. Niggah, I don't make a habit of repeating myself.

BOWZIE. Why can't *this* be college?

TONY. Brother, I'ma show you these hands—

BOWZIE. *(Sincerely.)* Don't let me be one of them uppity fools we
make fun of.

TONY. Aw, you know you too smart to let that happen.
That's why they let you in.

BOWZIE. Hell, I know I'm smart.
That's why I always act a fool. To hide it.

TONY. You a country Negro to your bones.

BOWZIE. I sure hope so.
I keep picturing them rich college kids and they fancy schools and
they fancy clothes.

TONY. Well you ain't go to no fancy grade school, but Sally made
the hell out of those threads.

BOWZIE. Sure did.

> *Beat.*

Hey, you ever heard of the Nashville Student Group.

TONY. I ain't been a student since I was ten. And wasn't a good one then.

Them kind of groups don't even know my name.

BOWZIE. Man in a suit dropped by yesterday inviting me to a meeting,

and, boy, it's a trip and a half.

He say "Is this the residence of Mr. Bow-Sigh Brandon?"

Just like that. Proper and all.

I thought it was a collector.

I almost slammed the door in his face except he was a Negro and wearing a suit.

TONY. Bow-Sigh?

BOWZIE. Just like that. "Mr. Bow-Sigh Brandon's residence."

TONY. Get out.

BOWZIE. I say, "Why yes indeed. I am *Prince* Bow-Sigh Brandon."

TONY. Hush your mouth.

BOWZIE. And he believed me!

TONY. That's gon' be you. *Prince Bow-Sigh Brandon!*

BOWZIE. Named James Lawson. One of them niggahs been riling up the ofays[6] at Woolworth's.

TONY. Them motherfuckers got too much time on their hands.

BOWZIE. You ain't never lied.

And Evelyn still mad we had to boycott for Easter and she couldn't get a Easter dress.

TONY. Sally, too.

BOWZIE. I told him:

I'm married

and trying study my way to good job so I can feed my family.

I ain't got time to be sitting at no diner counters.

And ain't even eating!

TONY. Just sitting there looking crazy.

BOWZIE. He say they ain't just sitting no more; they riding.

TONY. Riding?

6 An offensive term for a White person

BOWZIE. Buses.

TONY. What that got to do with anything?

BOWZIE. Say they riding down through Alabama.

TONY. For the hell of it?

BOWZIE. For the hell of it.

TONY. Boy!

BOWZIE. I say the only place my Black ass riding is the city bus to school and back.
I ain't got no time for that foolishness.

TONY. Educated Negros will find anything to be riled up about. For sure.

BOWZIE. For sure.

> *They breathe.*

I'm awfully sorry about the cake. I just get so full. I don't know what I'm doing with myself.

TONY. Go'n apologize, we alright. Ain't nobody hurt.

BOWZIE. *(An attempt at levity.)* Don't let me be one of them uppity fools we make fun of.

TONY. *(With levity.)* You already an uppity fool
and we already make fun of you.

BOWZIE. Man you ain't nothing.

TONY. Sure ain't.

> *They breathe easy. Sssss.*
> *And again. Sssss.*
> *And one more 'gain. Sssss.*

6

> *Bowzie holding a notebook.*
> *He's dressed to the nines but looking defeated.*

BOWZIE. Dearest Evelyn,

26

I'm writing you on the bus home from Fisk and...
Well, it's only been a week, and I'm already fearful this wasn't the right move, baby.

I'm writing because it's hard talking to you right about now.
I'm telling you, it's more than a notion.
Fisk University is only a handful of bus stops from our home but it's a whole damn world away.

I wish I could talk to you.
That you could hear me, I mean.
It ain't easy. Being your Bowzie.
Being out here being your Bowzie.
I wish I could be Tony sometimes.
Only thing I got on Tony is I can read my ABCs.
But I can't build things and work on cars like him.
I wish I could make you proud that way, but my hands don't work like that.
My head do.
Nobody would ever hire me for nothing Tony could do twice as good twice as fast.
I would've been a terrible slave, boy. Can you picture me? Under some fool's whip.
I'd say, "I'se workin' fast as I can, Massa!
But I sure could read your newspaper to you mighty quick!"

And I thought my head moved pretty quick. Thought I might be good at this.
This school thing, you know?
Something about being on campus
makes me feel like I need to shrink myself. Small as I can be.
They got all kinds of rich folks here. Rich Negros, I mean.
Met a fella from D.C. Boy got some sweet threads. Say his daddy is a lawyer.
A lawyer.
It's blowing my mind. Been to India.
I said, "Is that where the Indians from? I thought they was from Texas."
Everybody laughed real good on me for saying that.
I learned to go'n and be quiet after that.

27

Bowzie Brandon makes jokes just like the next man,
and just like the next man, he don't like being laughed at when he
ain't joking.

What I mean to say, Evelyn: I'm trying to be as small as I can,
which ain't something I can say I'm used to.

But I'm doing this for you.
I'm doing this for us.

I won't say any of this when this city bus drops me off and I walk
through that door.
When you fix dinner and ask me how my day went.
I'll say, "Fine."
And I'll tell you my suit look better than all them uppity fools.
We will laugh
and we'll make love
and we'll fall asleep in our bed.
And I'll wake up tomorrow to do it all over again.

One day I'll tell you this.
But for now…I'll hold on to this letter.
You'll read it when the time is right, I reckon.

All My Love,

Your Bowzie

7

> *Evelyn and Sally sit at the table playing a quiet game of gin
> rummy.*
>
> *Bowzie enters, stuffing a pamphlet into his jacket pocket.*

BOWZIE. Sorry, I'm late y'all.
The buses got held up.
EVELYN. Tony ain't back yet.
SALLY. Riffin' and raffin'.

> *Bowzie gives Evelyn a kiss.*

BOWZIE. Boss probably make him stay longer today.
The man would be able to call if y'all dish out the money for a telephone.

EVELYN. I guess we just thinking the worst.

SALLY. Hard to think something else when your husband here and mine ain't.

> *Without warning, Bowzie hops on the chair and begins singing a gospel song. The longer he sings, the more they realize he's doing a very exaggerated impersonation of Dr. Morgan Babb.**

(Remembering fondly.) The Pearl Cameron Singers.
My mama was wrong for putting me in that choir.

BOWZIE. Hush, now. I'm sanging.

> *He resumes his performance.*

EVELYN. Sing it, brother!

BOWZIE. And then they had the nerve to give Saddidy Sally-Mae Hargrow
—that's her maiden name, Hargrow—
the second solo.
Go'n, little Saddidy Sally-Mae. You still remember the words?

SALLY. I ain't fooling with you, man.

BOWZIE. Take it, Evelyn.

EVELYN. It's Sally's solo.

SALLY. My solo nothing. Whole church knew I couldn't sing worth a lick.
Everybody just making fun.
The only reason I was up in that choir
was so Mama could have her Wednesday nights free.

BOWZIE. *(In character again.)* I know somebody better get to sanging before the Holy Ghost go ahead and pass over.
Sang, Sister Evelyn!

> *Evelyn, not one to pass up an opportunity twice, finishes the song with a flourish. Her singing is even more exaggerated. Sally can't help but forget all about her troubles.*

And then like clockwork,
my mama would catch the spirit just like she practice at home.

SALLY. He a tale.

> *Bowzie catches the spirit like his mama.*

(Laughing.) You a big old tale!

BOWZIE. Evelyn know my mama practice.
Mama caught it at our wedding. I told the choir NO SLOW GOSPEL.
And what they do?
Some slow ass gospel.

EVELYN. Watch your mouth. You know Sally don't take no ugly words.

BOWZIE. Some sloowwwwww gospel.
I could just see Mama rearing up like a old mule
getting ready to have her moment in the sun.
Thank ya' Lawd! I thanks ya. I thanks ya!

EVELYN. A plum fool.

SALLY. He been like that ever since we were six.

BOWZIE. That's why they put me on the drums. Hoping I could run out of all that energy.

SALLY. Just gave him more.

BOWZIE. *(Re: Evelyn.)* 'Til I found this one.
Only one who had a mouth that could keep up with my legs.

EVELYN. Cut him down to size, that's all you needed.

BOWZIE. Well that ain't *all* I needed.

EVELYN. Boy, you better stop.

> *While they flirt, Sally goes to the door and looks out.*

He working, Sally. His firstborn nearly here.
A man got to work.

SALLY. Say he always working late, then how come I never see any more money?

> *Sally steps out to the porch.*
>
> *Evelyn and Bowzie are left alone.*

EVELYN. He not where he ain't supposed to be?
…Bowzie, you hear me talking to you.

BOWZIE. The man know he got a family.

EVELYN. That's your bosom buddy, I know that.

But he ain't the one you got to go home to.
His wife is fixing to have a fit.
You need to tell me:
He not where he ain't supposed to be, *right*?

BOWZIE. He stopped running with that gal a long time ago, Evelyn.
He's square now.
Jesus forgives.

EVELYN. Am I a White man with curly brown hair? Hell no.

BOWZIE. I done told you.

EVELYN. So my best friend is worried about nothing.
Right?

BOWZIE. She worrying for nothing.

EVELYN. Alright, Jack. Let me find out otherwise.

BOWZIE. See, why you gots to be so damn mean.

EVELYN. 'Cause if I was nice like Sally, you'd be running them
streets, too.

BOWZIE. And you'd be out there chasing me.

EVELYN. The hell I would.
I'd leave your ass so fast.
Let them raggedy heifers out there have you.

BOWZIE. *(Laughing.)* You wouldn't even put up a fight?

EVELYN. It's fight enough loving your crazy ass.

BOWZIE. Well that ain't how I feel.

EVELYN. Is that right?

BOWZIE. Nope. Loving you is easy as pie.

EVELYN. Hush, now.
I'm worried about her.
They used to be the picture of happiness.
Coretta and Martin couldn't hold a candle to those two.
Never a happier couple.

BOWZIE. Shoot, you talking like their love done withered and died.

EVELYN. Look at her.

BOWZIE. He coming home.

EVELYN. Where he *at*?

BOWZIE. Working.
The man is working.

EVELYN. He got that Chevy back.
What else he need?

BOWZIE. Baby, you know don't nothing stay the same.
That's how the world work.
Everything change.

EVELYN. Never liked change too much.

BOWZIE. He doing what he can, and she doing what she can.
They both doing their best.
Ain't that what matters?

EVELYN. What matters is that they happy.
And she ain't happy.

BOWZIE. Even if he doing something for his family—

EVELYN. It don't matter what the hell he doing if it ain't making his woman happy.

BOWZIE. Just 'cause she don't agree with it don't make it not for the family—

EVELYN. What the hell are you even talking about?

BOWZIE. *(Embracing her.)* Breathe, girl.

EVELYN. …Is something going on?

BOWZIE. What you mean?

EVELYN. Must be funny being around all those rich folk.

BOWZIE. No, it's fine.

EVELYN. Fine?

BOWZIE. Just fine.

EVELYN. Mhm.

> *Beat.*

I'm going out there.

> *They kiss.*
> *Evelyn exits.*
> *Bowzie is alone for a moment.*

He goes to Tony's stash.

He contributes a few bills.

He considers it.

He gives a few more dollars and then returns the stash to its hiding place.

8

BOWZIE. Dear Evelyn,

Pardon my handwriting.
The bus is more crowded than usual.
Today marks one whole month of summer classes.
My grades ain't too bad.
The schooling ain't the hard part...
The hard part...

> *He turns to a new sheet.*

Evelyn,

There's a reason I've been coming home late from class every night this week.
It's hard to say, but I want to tell you because...
Because I think you should know where my head has been these days.
Sometime I get so used to being real strong
or real funny
that being real sad don't fit to my character like it probably should.

Or telling you something serious:

These school Negros...
They invited me to a night meeting.
And I figure if I was ever gonna get a shot at moving up in life,
then this is how I gotta do it.
So, I went.
They talk real big talk.
I understand why Negros been kept from around books.
Mess around and start talking like this.

(Imitating.) About rights
and what's legal and why the law should be upheld.
Why they gotta demonstrate and the definition of the word:
de mon strate.

And, I'll be honest, it all sounds right pretty.
It all sounds like it make a whole lot of sense.
I thought picking a major and getting me a degree
was gonna be the most important thing I ever did next to marrying you.

But I'm starting to feel like maybe this was just a step toward something else.
Toward something real different than what I thought…

Seem like this the sort of thing I should say out loud. I just don't know when.

>   *He balls up the letter.*

9

>   *Evening.*
>   *Tony and Sally are entering and reentering the room as they dress for church. Tony stops and watches Sally for a moment.*
>   *He lets out a huge sigh.*
>   *Sally ignores him.*
>   *He lets out another sigh.*
>   *Sally grins and ignores him.*
>   *Before Tony can sigh again—*

SALLY. Long day at work, Tony?
I know you ain't too tired to praise the Lord on *this* Summer Revival?
TONY. Naw naw naw.
It's only Monday.
SALLY. Precisely.
TONY. Got Tuesday,

Wednesday,
Thursday,
Friday,
Saturday night,
and Sunday morning to make it through.

SALLY. Mhm.

TONY. Too early in the week to be tired.

SALLY. That's right.

> *Beat.*

TONY. It's just that I ain't never seen the point in Summer Revival.
Same sermon, same choir, same everything
'cept we in a tent five times hotter, ten times as loud, and twenty
times more crying.

SALLY. Tony, that tie don't match.
You dress nicer for the number house than you do for the house of
God.

TONY. 'Cause it's hot in that tent!

SALLY. It's hotter in hell.

TONY. Says you.
I'd like to take me a thermometer and check myself.

SALLY. Do we need a reminder lesson about why you *promised* to go
to Revival with me—

TONY. Sally, come on, baby. I'm teasing is all.
I am over the moon to be going to Revival with my beautiful, loving,
forgiving wife.

SALLY. Good, 'cause if you need reminding, I can sure 'nough teach
it.

TONY. I know you can.
And you know your husband is just fine giving up a whole week's
worth of night pay *just* to hear Watkins hoopin'
and see Sister Shaw and Sister Brinkley sing every song they know.

SALLY. The tie.

TONY. Yes, ma'am.

SALLY. And you best not laugh when Aunt[7] Faye get happy and start running.

Last time, you embarrassed me so bad I thought I was gonna die.

TONY. Tell your aunt she got too much bosom to be doing all that running.

And got the nerve to sit in the middle of the aisle.

At least three men still got knots on they head from those knockers!

SALLY. Ooh, the devil gon' get you.

> *Evelyn storms into the Carters' home abruptly.*
>
> *She is followed by Bowzie, who is attempting not to have this fight in the Carter's home, but is quickly unsuccessful.*

EVELYN. Y'all talk some sense into him!

BOWZIE. *(Quieting.)* Evelyn Brandon, I told you don't be bothering—

EVELYN. I didn't get my Easter dress thanks to those niggahs and that godforsaken boycott and now they got my husband.

BOWZIE. They don't care nothing about yo' dress.

EVELYN. My poppa pride himself ain't no crackers ever burn down his house

or throw no bricks through his window,

and you gon' knock out like this?

SALLY. What is going on?

EVELYN. He killing himself. I married a fool of a niggah. Just killing hisself.

BOWZIE. You can't see I'm doing this for you?

EVELYN. For me?!
The hell you are.

BOWZIE. Who else I'm doing it for, huh?

EVELYN. How should I know?
How on God's earth should I know why you—
Why you just dangling your scrawny Black ass in front of the Klan?

SALLY. *Evelyn.*

EVELYN. I ain't gonna mince words, Sally.
What this *niggah* doing is truly beyond me.

7 Pronounced "Ain't"

BOWZIE. It's not a sit-in. We ain't breaking the law. It's legal.

EVELYN. Throwing your life away.
Your education!
What about your family?!

BOWZIE. I ain't no paw[8] yet.

TONY. You ain't going to school?

EVELYN. And you ain't never gonna be no paw,
hopping on that bus 'cross the country.
A damn fool.

SALLY. Bus?

EVELYN. Tell 'em.
Tell 'em what you walked in and told me!
Coming home every night acting like everything's just fine
then tell me this out the blue.
Sally-Mae, you might as well take that suit on back; you gon' need
it for his funeral.

BOWZIE. Woman, I done had it up to here—

EVELYN. You already saw what happened.
Them fools got whooped 'bout to death in Birmingham on Mother's
Day
and had to fly a plane outta there to freedom. Not a bus in sight—

BOWZIE. And that's *exactly* why we gotta keep riding.
Klan and Coke bottles can't stop us from following the law.
We got a role in this thing.
I can make sure the words and ideas in the Constitution ain't just
pretty thoughts—

EVELYN. You don't even sound like yourself.
Let them niggahs brainwash you is what you sound like.

SALLY. Hush now!!!

        Quiet.

Y'all loud and riling my little girl up.
What is the commotion?

TONY. You dropping out?

BOWZIE. I'm taking me a little break.

TONY. *(Incredulous.)* A little break.

EVELYN. He a lie.
Fisk say if he go on them rides, he quitting school.

BOWZIE. Now listen here, y'all. I thought it through.
Ain't no use in sitting up in those classes if I'm the only one there.

TONY. You going on them buses?

SALLY. The Freedom Rides we saw in the paper?
Where the police let that mob attack those folks?
You're gonna go on a Freedom Ride?

BOWZIE. Y'all...

> *Beat.*

SALLY. ...we waiting.

BOWZIE. We just going to Jackson and to—

TONY. Jackson, Mississippi?!
Mississippi?!

BOWZIE. Just to Jackson and New Orleans and back.

EVELYN. New Orleans?!

TONY. Niggah, you won't make it past Chattanooga!

EVELYN. He won't make it past Mount Juliet!

SALLY. You sure about this, Bowzie?

EVELYN. Sally—

SALLY. You sure about this, Bowzie?

BOWZIE. There's gonna be White folks and Coloreds alike.
It's a peaceful protest.

SALLY. Peaceful...
Tony.
Evelyn.
Bowzie say he taking up with a peaceful protest.
You sure it's gonna be peaceful?
White folks and Coloreds alike? They gon' let you sit at the front of the bus?

BOWZIE. Sit wherever we please. Evelyn, baby—

EVELYN. Don't talk to me, man.

SALLY. Evelyn.

Tony.

We wanted our Bowzie Brandon to do something with his life,
and that's what he's doing.

Right, Bowzie?

You making something out of your life,
that right?

BOWZIE. That's right. That's what I'm doing.

> *Sally takes Evelyn's hands.*

SALLY. Your Bowzie Brandon got more brains than the three of us
put together.

He got enough sense to know what might happen if he hop on that
bus.

(To Bowzie.) Don't he?

> *Bowzie breathes.*

(Truly concerned.) Don't he?

BOWZIE. Yes, ma'am.

SALLY. *(To Bowzie.)* He know they might do nasty things to him.

Say nasty things to him.

Be awful to him and everybody on that bus.

He know they might try to kill
everybody on that bus.

He *know* that.

Don't he?

BOWZIE. *(To Evelyn.)* He do.

SALLY. *(To Tony.)* And right now him and Tony gonna go off on a
little walk

and make sure Bowzie Brandon got a good plan

so me and Mrs. Bowzie Brandon can have some lady talk.

Ain't that right?

TONY. Yes, ma'am.

> *The men exit.*

SALLY. Evelyn.

EVELYN. Sally-Mae.

SALLY. It's gonna be alright—

EVELYN. He is, Sally. He is.

SALLY. Is?

EVELYN. He *is* a paw.
He's gonna be a daddy.

SALLY. *(Joyfully.)* My Lord!
You sure?

EVELYN. I ain't gon' tell him.

SALLY. Evelyn.

EVELYN. I'll be damned if I tell him.
I know you love him like a brother, but you can't tell him, Sally.

SALLY. Shhh.

EVELYN. I'll be damned if I tell him.

SALLY. You don't have to tell him nothing you don't want to.

EVELYN. You didn't know me before Bowzie, but I was something
like a wild woman.
Sanging was all I needed. Didn't need no husband.
Me, God, and the microphone got along just fine on our own.
That's why the circuit treat me so good.
Not normal to have a woman sing like an angel, drink like a man,
and keep her legs closed like a lady.
Folks liked that.
And lessin'[9] I got real lonely,
beer and bid whist[10] was the only man-company I needed.

When you introduced me to Bowzie,
that was the first time having babies even crossed my mind.
If that old Evelyn could see me now, she'd have a right laugh.
Me crying to my girlfriend 'cause my husband left me with a baby—

SALLY. Hush.

EVELYN. I ain't lying.
Messing up my face over a man 'cause I got my mind fixed on a great
big house with a whole mess of children—

9 Unless

10 The best card game ever

40

Listen to me.
This ain't me.

SALLY. We grow.
You ain't nothing but a flower getting a little rain.
You thought you had already growed as tall as you was gonna grow,
but a flower can't bloom on sun alone. Take a little rain.

EVELYN. Come on, now.

SALLY. Listen to somebody who done had they fair share of rain.
And Bowzie need to grow, too.
He need his own rain to grow the way God called him.
You gots to thank God for the rain as well as the sunshine, now.
You ain't no rundown woman with a no-good man who done run
off on you.
That's a situation I know a little bit about, hm?

> *Evelyn nods.*

You a woman with a good man who knows he got a good thing.
You a good thing, girl.

EVELYN. I sure am.
We *both* good things.

SALLY. Amen to that. Amen to that.
Now, more importantly,
my little girl's gonna have a playmate!

EVELYN. Oh, hush, girl. I can't believe I even told you.

SALLY. What took you so long?

EVELYN. Just scared, I guess.
Wanted to keep it a secret 'til I knew it was real.

SALLY. Of course it's real!
You are pregnant with a beautiful, healthy, amazing gift from God.

> *Beat.*

(Sing-song.) *Evelyn's having a ba-by,*
Evelyn's having a ba-by!

EVELYN. Hush.

SALLY. Sing it with me, girl. You know I sound crazy.
Evelyn's having a ba-by,
Evelyn's having a ba-by!

EVELYN. *(Giggling in spite of herself.)* Just as afflicted as you wanna be.

SALLY. Don't talk about me. Sing with me.
Evelyn's having a ba-by,

EVELYN. *(With her, reluctantly.)* Evelyn's having a ba-by.

> *Their singing dissolves into a soft silence before the men enter.*

TONY. We back.

EVELYN. We see.

SALLY. Y'all ready for church?

> *Sally walks to Tony's side.*
>
> *Bowzie goes halfway to Evelyn, then gets on one knee.*
>
> *Evelyn tries to ignore him, but Bowzie is so sad and so very afraid.*
>
> *Evelyn meets Bowzie halfway.*

EVELYN. Let's get on to Revival.

> *Evelyn exits.*
>
> *Bowzie exits.*
>
> *Tony exits.*
>
> *Sally exits.*
>
> *The Pretty Green Chevy revs up and then drives off.*

10

> *We see Tony alone.*
> *Tony is a hard man.*
> *We watch Tony.*
> *Tony has a soft touch.*
> *We really see Tony.*
> *Tony is really trying.*

11

The light of Sunday morning shines on the quiet and empty house. It's almost as beautiful as when we first encountered it, but something's changed. Something we can't quite place.

Suddenly and surprisingly, all four of them reenter, having a ball!

BOWZIE. *(Hooping like Pastor Watkins.)* They *buried* Him Friday night. *Ha!*
He stayed in the grave all night Friday,
He stayed in that grave all night Saturday. *Ha-ha!*
But earllllllly Sunday morning.
(Ain't God alright?)
Earllllllly Sunday morning,
On a Sunday morning much like this Sunday morning today.
He got up with all power in His hands!
Glory!
I'm gon' tell y'all like Granny told me:
Ninety-nine!!!

> *Deep and loud gasp for air.*

and a half

> *Same deep gasp.*

won't do!

> *Same deep gasp.*

Sometimes

> *Same deep gasp.*

I'm down

> *Same deep gasp.*

and sometimes

> *Same deep gasp.*

I'm up.

> *Same deep gasp.*

But thanks ya Lawd!

I'm gon' run on.
Are you gonna run on?
'Cause I'm gonna run onnnnnnn

> *Same deep gasp.*

And see what the end gon' be.
Take it away, Brother Rutherford!

> *Bowzie points at Tony.*

> *Tony begins to sing a gospel song. As he sings, he stomps to keep the rhythm. All join in at the chorus.*

EVELYN. And then Sister Brinkley be trying to compete,
'cause you know she mad Sister Shaw got the praise and worship song!

> *Evelyn imitates Sister Brinkley singing.*

> *Tony and Evelyn compete with singing tricks for the remainder of the song. The moment is playful and entertaining, but also moving. They believe the words they sing. They love the people they imitate. It is beautiful.*

BOWZIE. *(Imitating Pastor Watkins.)* Mother Scrivens.
Come on up here.
Give us the benediction.
(In his regular voice.) Now you know she move slow as molasses.
(Imitating Pastor Watkins.) Take your time, Mother Scrivens.

SALLY. *(Imitating Mother Scrivens.)* I'm on my way, baby.
Well, you know. The old lady's doing 'bout the same,
fair to middling.
But my good days
outweigh my bad days.

EVELYN. Sound just like her!

> *As Sally delivers the benediction, their moment becomes less playful and more sincere. The words mean something as they land on the four friends.*

SALLY. *(Imitating Mother Scrivens.)* And I just wanna say,
"May the Lord bless ya.
And keeps ya.
And make His face shine upon ya.

And always be gracious to ya.
Lord lift you high and count on ya and give you peace.
Bless your coming
and your going,
on the highways and on the byways.
And a special prayer for Li'l Bowzie Brandon.
He hopping on the Freedom Ride tomorrow. Fighting for his rights.
Offer a special protecting.
And let the church says:
Amen."

ALL. Amen.

> *The silence slowly becomes weighted by awareness that this very well might be the last moment like this they'll have. The silence holds and wraps around each of them individually.*

> *This moment takes a long,   long time.*

> *Evelyn wipes a tear quickly, then storms away.*

BOWZIE. Well, I guess I best get packed for tomorrow.
(To Tony.) Pick me up in the morning?

> *Tony exits.*

> *Bowzie looks to Sally, who looks to the ground.*

We had a nice week.
The four of us.
Together every night for Revival.
Evelyn gave up her shifts at Lark's Juke Joint,
and she'd just about roll over and die before she misses out on that
weekend money.
And Tony actually showing up on time.

> *Sally chuckles politely.*

Sally, it's been a right nice week.
Hasn't it…?

SALLY. …Yeah. It has.

BOWZIE. I feel good about this.

SALLY. Have you talked to Evelyn?

BOWZIE. She just been pretending like it ain't happening.

SALLY. She hasn't said anything?

BOWZIE. She come home, we go to Revival, we go to bed.

SALLY. You best to talk to her.

BOWZIE. Yeah.

SALLY. I mean it, Bowzie.

BOWZIE. *(Lightening the mood.)* Hey, you know what you oughta do?

SALLY. What's that?

BOWZIE. Show up to Fisk tomorrow morning.
Take you the city bus right on down to the school stop at 9 A.M.

SALLY. What for?

BOWZIE. Tell them your name is Bowzie Brandon.
I can see it now.
Wear you one of Tony's good suits.
Hide all that hair under one of his hats.
Go'n and get that degree for me.
Shoot, you always made better grades than me.
Get you two degrees.
One for Glamour School *and* one for Fisk Uni—

SALLY. *(Harrowed.)* That ain't funny.
That ain't funny one bit.

BOWZIE. What if I'm not being funny?—

SALLY. You can't joke this away.
You can't "funny" your way out of this.
If you hop on that Greyhound bus—

BOWZIE. *When* I get on that Greyhound, it'll be the first serious thing I've done in my life.

> *Sally looks at Bowzie hard.*
>
> *Bowzie doesn't waver under her gaze.*

I mean it.
For the first time in my life.
I finally looked around, and I can't stop seeing it…

How humiliating it really is to walk around my own town without basic human dignity.

SALLY. Dignit—

BOWZIE. Let me finish.

I'm not trying to be ugly.

And I'm so proud of us.

No jive.

I am proud as all get-out of the life we've made where we can feel safe.

And happy.

And fall in love.

And get a little piece of this American Experiment for ourselves.

But that ain't justice.

What we doing, Sally, it ain't justice.

And I got a chance…to help grab us some true justice.

More than just a tiny piece of the dream.

I don't care if they call me an agitator.

I don't care if they kill me.

I don't.

If I die.

Sally, look at me.

Please.

If I do die on this journey.

Then you'll be able to put every single letter of my name on my tombstone:

Bowzie Buchanan Brandon.

Because my name will mean something.

My life will have meant something.

But if I stay…to make y'all happy.

Well, I could live a hundred years

and y'all'll still have to leave my tombstone empty.

'Cause my name would be worthless.

Even if nobody but you, Evelyn, and Tony remember my name.

I want it to mean *something* when I go on to Glory.

    Beat.

SALLY. I've always looked at you like a little brother, you know that.
This moment right now.

I see a man.

Be safe.

(Sternly.) And talk to Evelyn.

If she don't want to talk now, she will.

Call her.

BOWZIE. I will.

SALLY. Ain't nobody dying.

God protects the Faithful.

God protects, you hear me?

> *Sally and Bowzie hug.*
>
> *Bowzie gives Sally's belly a rub for good measure.*
>
> *Bowzie lingers.*
>
> *Sally knows what he's thinking.*

Go'n now.

Everything will be right here when you get back.

Just as you left it.

> *Bowzie kisses Sally on the cheek before exiting.*
>
> *Sally stands, steeling herself.*

End of Act One

ACT TWO

1

A brand-new morning.
Sally stands with her toes feeling the fresh morning dew.
She is waiting.
Sally takes a deep breath. A gentle: Huh!
The Pretty Green Chevy draws near and parks.
Tony enters. A wide, deep gulf exists between them.
They both wait for the other to speak.
Tony walks past Sally into the house.
Sally follows.

SALLY. He on the bus?

TONY. Yep.

SALLY. …Good.

> *Beat.*

You want some breakfast or something before you head off to work?
I can whip up some grits real quick or a couple biscuits you can take
with you?

TONY. *(Almost to himself.)* Bowzie and I met when I was ten. He
my first and only friend.

SALLY. Attached at the hip—

TONY. Look like he gon' be my last one, too.

SALLY. *(Commanding.)* Don't you dare say that.

> *Tony doesn't respond.*

Tony Carter, you hear me talking to you.

TONY. What?!

SALLY. …I swear 'fore God, I know you feel rotten
but the most you got in your power is to support him

and pray for him 'til he get back.

He left but I am here. It is just me and you and your daughter…

> *Sally presents her belly to Tony.*
>
> *Tony refuses to look.*

All hell will break loose when Tony Carter's firstborn enters this world.

And you have got to be here for it.

TONY. Sally-Mae.

SALLY. Let me finish, please.

TONY. Fine.

SALLY. I let you slide between young and country and foolish but not with no child.

TONY. Leave me be.

SALLY. No. I ain't.

That's how we ended up where we at.

Me leaving you be.

Me watching you drift on away, and just pretending you loved me enough to stay.

TONY. Where I'm at?

SALLY. A million miles away, blaming it on Bowzie.

TONY. Blaming it on Bowzie?—

SALLY. You are a father. I need you here.

I need you to stay with me.

TONY. I ain't going a goddamn place, woman.

SALLY. Watch your mouth!

TONY. Sally-Mae, you gonna let me be human?!

You gon' let me mess up without me living my life with a collar around my neck?!

SALLY. She came to my job, Tony.

TONY. You don't think I know that?

SALLY. *(Snapping.)* You ain't acting like it.

You ain't acting like just last summer, I didn't walk out of my job to see that woman.

That woman I *knew* deep in my gut existed.

50

In my face.

Telling me she need to talk to me and she'll walk me home—

TONY. Stop riling yourself up—

SALLY. *(A plea.)* Where have you been at night?!

You wouldn't need no collar if you would just come home at night.

TONY. *(Snapping back.)* You said it yourself

I'm a father.

So if the foreman say I gotta work a little later to get my full rate,

you bet your ass I'ma say "Yessuh, massa" and get to work.

Now leave it be.

SALLY. Tony—

TONY. Goddammit, leave it be!!!

> *Tony erupts.*
>
> *It's explosive.*
>
> *It's scary.*
>
> *The audience wants to duck for cover.*
>
> *He grabs whatever he needs for work before leaving and slamming the door behind him.*
>
> *The Chevy revs up and drives off.*
>
> *Slowly, Sally begins fixing whatever Tony may have broken. Maybe it's a beer bottle, maybe it's the radio, most likely it's one of their four chairs. Whatever it is, it can be fixed. So, she fixes it the best she can.*
>
> *As she is putting the pieces back together,*

2

> *Bowzie on a Greyhound bus.*
>
> *We hear the chanting of angry "protestors" surrounding the bus.*
>
> *We can feel his fear.*
>
> *Eventually, he pulls out a notebook.*

BOWZIE. Dear Sally,

We made it to Jackson.

The bus is stopped because they're trying to figure out what to do with us.

Won't let us keep heading on to New Orleans.

We been sitting here what feels like forever…

We passed by thirty-eight burning crosses.

I know because I counted them.

The Mother's Day bus folks said they don't know how they made it off the bus alive.

Well we alive but…I'll be straight with you.

I don't know for how much longer.

I'm writing you 'cause I been calling Evelyn ever since we left.

Just like you told me.

She won't pick up.

I'm 'bout out of nickels.

Last time I seen her it was with a cast-iron skillet flying toward my head.

I know you don't like secrets, but please don't tell her I wrote you.

Every time I fix my mind to write her a letter, it just doesn't feel right.

It feels like we should talk…really communicate.

But maybe it's too late for that…

I'm just hoping that the first time Evelyn hear from me, it'll be my voice.

But she won't pick up the telephone.

I ain't no coward, Sally.

You known me longer than anybody,

and you know I'm a lot of things, but I ain't a coward.

I'm starting to think Evelyn was right in calling me a fool, though.

More I talk to everybody, more I realize I'm the poorest Negro here.

I made friends with a brother named Matthew.

His daddy is the richest Negro doctor in Nashville!

You know Matthew Walker Health Center? That's his daddy!

The whole world think we just a mess of down and out, honkey tonk Negroes when really I'm the only one!

Anyway.
Sally, hold on to this letter.
I miss y'all already.

All the way from the deep deep South,

Bowzie

P.S.:
The green trunk in the shed…there are a couple of letters.
And a will.
Left everything to Evelyn.
It's legally binding in case it come to that.
She won't need it. But in case she does.

3

> *Evelyn in the Carters' home. The small world in her womb is beginning to show. She looks at the door, half-wondering if Bowzie will enter.*
>
> *Of course, he doesn't.*
>
> *Evelyn takes out a bundle from her purse to continue knitting baby clothes.*
>
> *She knits one particular stitch.*
>
> *She does it and undoes it.*
>
> *Over and over again.*

EVELYN. God damn it!

> *Tony enters.*

TONY. Hey, hey!
Hey now!

EVELYN. God—

TONY. Heyyyyyy.
Shhhh.

EVELYN. I just.

TONY. Calm down!

EVELYN. I'm sorry to be a nuisance.
I just can't be at that empty house any longer.

TONY. Who say you a nuisance.
Hush, girl.
You alright?

EVELYN. No, I'm not alright, Tony.
Far from it!
I am as far from alright as can be.

TONY. What's the matter?

EVELYN. Tony.
Why is he so dumb? Why is he just so foolish!
Just a damn fool.

TONY. It's okay.

EVELYN. It's "okay"?
Do you know what I had to do today?
This morning.
All by myself.
I had to go to the doctor and have him check my belly.
Alone.
Me sitting up in that doctor's office looking like a…
Like a…
Like damn harlot!

TONY. Come here, come here.

> *They embrace.*

EVELYN. I'm gonna have to raise my baby alone.

TONY. *(An attempt at levity.)* Look, I know you all argued something awful before he left. He told me.

EVELYN. *(With levity.)* I threw a frying pan at him.

TONY. You threw a frying pan at him.
And almost got him.

EVELYN. Damn right.

TONY. But you didn't.
He ducked clear out of that frying pan's way,
and he's gonna duck whatever these crackers throw at him.

On the way, he told me the worst was over: That Kennedy boy's involved and all.

EVELYN. The devil is a lie.

TONY. It's the truth.

EVELYN. How he know?
How some podunk Negro
from backwoods Nashville
know a damn thing 'bout what *President* Jack Kennedy doing?
He don't!
He a fool if ever was one, and I don't want nothing to do with him.
Nothing.

TONY. You can't see no value in it?

EVELYN. You really asking me that? Like you don't already know my answer.

TONY. Evelyn. No value?

EVELYN. Not a lick!
What the hell good he gon' do getting hisself killed?
Just selfish.
You know what got value, Tony? What got value is schooling
like Sally
or a trade like you.
All that man had going for him was he smart as a whip
and could make me giggle so hard my clothes just fall off.
That's all.
I make the money.
Me.
Even when I quit the circuit and stayed in Nashville.
My singing is what keeps a roof over his head and food in his belly.
It's *his* turn!
His turn to keep a roof over my head and food in my belly.
Asking me if I see any value.
That man ain't got no value to me unless he in my bed or in somebody's classroom.

TONY. He your husband—

EVELYN. No, he ain't.
He just some niggah already in the grave far as I'm concerned.

TONY. Don't be wishing death on—

EVELYN. I told Sally the same thing when *you* couldn't get your life right.

TONY. *(Commanding.)* Leave me out of this, Evelyn.

EVELYN. Naw, you in it.
I made Sally say those very words to me: "He—is—dead—to—me."
Negro woman will follow Satan to the grave
long as Satan's dressed up like a black man
and some preacher tell her it's God's will.

My mama gave my daddy twelve children
only to have a woman half her age come to the door one day
—Thanksgiving Day—
and say, "That's *my* man."
Say, "I been screwing your husband,
and I'm tired of spending holidays alone."
And do you know my daddy went with her?
After twelve children, he walked out on my mama.
And when the heifer left my daddy, my mama took his ass back.
You in it too, Tony. You and your friend dragging your women through the mud
'cause we the only ones who take those vows seriously.

TONY. Where am I now, Evelyn? Huh?
Who's doing Sally wrong, huh?
You mad at your mama 'cause your daddy made a mistake.
But where your daddy at, huh?
Sound to me like your daddy raised twelve children
and had one mistake you won't let him live down.

EVELYN. Oh, why just bless your heart.
That's what you call a mistake?
A mistake is drinking too much at the bar.
Or playing the numbers and losing your paycheck.
Throwing your family away ain't no mistake.
That whore you screwed
while Sally was here thinking her husband walk on water—

TONY. *(Booming.)* Woman!!!

EVELYN. *NEGRO* woman! That's what you mean.

56

Negro woman.

That's the difference. Except far as I can tell, Negro *men* a rare breed. Hell, "men" too nice a word. Y'all *boys*! Black *boys*!

TONY. This ain't about me, "Negro woman"!

EVELYN. It is.

The both of you.

Him charming as all get-out and you just winking at any young thing in a skirt walk by.

Everybody knows it was more than just that one heifer who showed up to Sally's job.

You throw away your marriage.

Bowzie throw away his life.

While I never knew there was a difference.

It's about your ass too, boy.

You and Bowzie both.

Well you ain't the only two who can throw your weight around.

You ain't the only two who can just behave any kind of way you want.

You ain't the only two who get to forget about your vows;

do whatever the hell you want.

> *Evelyn kisses Tony.*

> *Shit.*

(Trying not to cry.) See?

Ain't that hard.

Throwing everything away—

> *Evelyn exits.*

> *Tony goes to his stash of money and holds it.*

4

> *Bowzie, bare chest, in underdrawers.*

BOWZIE. Whelp, Sally. I'm in jail.

Jail number two, actually.

They locked us up in Jackson.

Formal charges:

"Incitement to riot.
Breach of peace.
And failure to obey a police officer."
But six days later the jail filled up.
Dozens of folks hopped directly off the bus into the jail.
From all over the country.
So many they didn't have any more room.
So they had to move us!
And now, Parchman State Prison Farm.

When we got here,
we went into a room a few at a time.
Made me sit in a chair.
There was a deputy behind me, a deputy to my right, and a deputy
to my left.
Each deputy had blackjacks.
And the deputy behind the desk told each of us,
"I'ma ask you some questions. Can you answer 'Yes, sir' or 'No, sir'?"
And it didn't take long to put together
that the deputies with the blackjacks
were there to hit you in case you failed to say "sir."

That's how they introduced us to Parchman Penitentiary.
Making sure we know they the boss.

This is…challenging.

And it ain't just coming from the Whites.
Damn Uncle Toms.
A group of Colored men
came by the jail window one morning.

Jailers let people visit like that from time to time
if they saying something they want us to hear.
They say, "You folks are brave.
You'll probably win desegregation.
But put the idea of reparations out your mind."
You believe that, Sally?

I didn't want to write you from jail.
I figured if Evelyn got hold of the letters, I didn't want her knowing

…but…

…How is she?

Can you ask her to pick up the telephone?

I'm the only one here who ain't talked to his family.

5

> *Night. Tony is staring into the distance, holding a beer. Sally walks from the back room, behind him. Turns on a light.*

SALLY. That you, Tony Carter?

> *Tony is silent.*

You gon' be tired all day. Not fit for work if you don't get you some rest.

> *Tony is silent.*

I bet that beer is warm, ain't it?

I bet you ain't take two good sips, have you?

TONY. I don't like the taste.

SALLY. Then why you holding it?

TONY. That's what you do when you sad. Drink.

SALLY. Who say you got to drink a beer?

Get you a cold drink. Something you gonna finish at least.

TONY. Sure 'nough?

SALLY. *(An attempt at levity.)* Just wasting money.

TONY. Why don't you finish it?

SALLY. I don't want your warm beer, man.

> *Beat.*

TONY. Man yell at a pregnant woman oughta be locked up.

SALLY. I ain't gonna argue with you on that.

TONY. I shouldn't have done that.

Losing my temper, being sad, that girl, all of it.

I shouldn't have done that none of that.

SALLY. Alright.

TONY. Sally, I ain't riffin' and raffin'.

SALLY. Mm.

TONY. You gots to know that.
I cut all that loose.
And the day I found out you was expecting, I played my last number.

SALLY. Hush.

TONY. I ain't lying.
I went right down to the number house and told them
if I don't hit today, I ain't never gonna hit.
Said, "This here is my last number. I got a child to raise now.
I can't be throwing my money away like that no more."

SALLY. And what happened?
Did you hit?

TONY. Naw. Lord didn't see fit.

SALLY. You know I worked real hard on you, Tony Carter.

TONY. What you mean?

SALLY. *(Reminiscing.)* I worked mighty hard on you.
Soon as you and all your little country cousins come
picking girls off the hayride and you picked me,
I knew I was gonna have to work hard not to be one of those girls.
One of those girls who get knocked up without a husband
and gotta stand in front of the whole church to apologize and repent.
You got my stomach twirling soon as I met you,
but I wasn't gonna apologize and repent for nobody.

TONY. Oh, don't I know it.

SALLY. I did all that work for you. And I hoped to God you'd be
willing to work for me.

TONY. I told you I cut all that loose. I quit that girl
and I quit all the foolishness.

SALLY. *(Gently.)* And I'm telling you I didn't have no foolishness to
quit.

TONY. What else can I do, Sally?
I went to Revival like I promised. I hardly miss one Sunday a month.
I work overtime.
What do you want?

SALLY. I want...you to come back to bed where you belong.
Instead of staring out at the world.

TONY. I ain't staring at the world.

SALLY. What's out there in the world that you gotta stare at that ain't right here?

TONY. I'm staring out there looking for Bowzie.
It's like I don't know which way is up.
I don't know whether to check my behind or scratch my watch.

SALLY. Bowzie is exactly where he belong. You need to be where you belong.

TONY. Where I belong...

SALLY. Where you belong...

> *Beat.*

Come on to bed.
Please.

> *Tony follows her to bed.*

6

BOWZIE. *(Trying with all of his might.)* Hey, Sally.
I'm writing this letter on a paper towel 'cause they won't give us no paper.
Ain't much to say.
It don't seem like things are getting much better.
But we're all in good spirits.
Singing freedom songs even when the guards tell us to stop.
Sharing stories, meeting folks.
They say there are hundreds of folks jailed here.
Round three hundred, in fact.
From all over.
D.C., Florida, Chicago.
Blacks, Whites, Jews.
It ain't so bad.
It ain't so bad...

Evelyn stands at a microphone in a stunning dress.

EVELYN. Thank y'all for having me back tonight.
Seem like I'm in this juke joint more often now than when Lark first made me a regular.
You remember them days, Lark?
I was a little younger then, wasn't I? Before these hips grew in.
Anyway, I hope y'all ain't bored with me yet.
I appreciate y'all keeping me company and hope I'm doing alright returning the favor.
Here's a number I heard the other day and just can't get out of my head.
Curtis?
Curtis! Go'n 'head and bring in the bottom.

> *Evelyn begins to sing a torch number. She is hypnotic as she sings; however, she is mourning.*

(*Singing.*) *Look at that tiny, broken bird*
> *Look at her sitting, staring at the sky*
> *Look, her wing is broken*
> *Her golden feathers*
> *Shimmer in the light*

> *From a distance, I couldn't see*
> *That this little bird was just like me*

> *Whoa, she cannot fly*
> *She cannot fly*
> *She cannot fly*
> *She cannot fly*
> *She cannot fly*

> *Look at that tiny bird*
> *Look at her sitting, cursing to the sky*
> *Look, her wing is broken*
> *Her feet are planted*
> *She's putting up a fight*

From a distance, I couldn't see
That this little bird was just like me

Whoa, she cannot fly
She cannot fly
She cannot fly
She cannot fly

Look at that tiny, broken bird
Look, she's cursed the sky for just bein' the sky
Look, she won't curse her broken wing
She is broken
She cannot fly

From a distance, I couldn't see
That this little bird was just like me

    During the song, we hear Bowzie singing a Freedom Song.

    We hear Sally singing a church song.

    We hear Tony singing a work song.

    The band continues to play as Evelyn cries at the microphone.

BOWZIE. *(Singing.) She's gonna fly*

EVELYN. *(Singing.) So she curses the sky*

TONY. *(Singing.) She's gonna fly*

EVELYN. *(Singing.) So she curses the sky*

SALLY. *(Singing.) She's gonna fly*

EVELYN. *(Singing.) She curses the sky*

BOWZIE, TONY, and SALLY. *(Singing.) She's gonna fly*

8

BOWZIE. I'm going crazy.
Like my mind don't belong to me no more.
I'm in this cell with mice.
Thirty-two days.
Mice.
Mice and mice shit.

Everywhere.
And roaches.
And…and dirty mattresses.
Most the folks I came with already been bailed out…
I miss my bed.
I miss you and Tony.
I miss Evelyn.
Sally, I want to go home.
I'm scared that…
I'm scared she won't be there when I get back…
I can't sleep.
I'm losing my mind, Sally.

9

Tony is scratching at his leg voraciously when Evelyn enters.

TONY. Oh.

EVELYN. I'm sorry; I just swung by real fast to drop these off for Sally—

TONY. You ain't gotta explain yourself. *(Re: his leg.)* Goddamn chiggers.[11]

EVELYN. Just put some nail varnish on it.

TONY. Nail varnish? What I want with a red leg?

EVELYN. *(Rummaging through her purse.)* It come in clear, too.
Chiggers dig in deep but if you apply some nail varnish,
they can't breathe too good.
Next thing you know, you chigger-free.

TONY. How you learn so much?

EVELYN. Had eleven brothers and sisters. Got real good at tending other folks' childrens.

TONY. You gon' be a good mama.

    Beat.

EVELYN. *(Re: the nail varnish.)* I don't have to if you don't want me to.

11 Barely visible mites that live in grass brushes and burrow into one's skin causing an awful itch

Tony contemplates.

He rolls his trousers' leg up and steps his foot on a chair for Evelyn.

Evelyn contemplates.

She applies nail varnish to the chigger bites.

How you get these anyway? You supposed to be working construction this week.

TONY. I picked up a little extra work at MacHenry's farm early morning.

EVELYN. Working *late*…working *early*…

TONY. Don't see how that make you no difference.

EVELYN. Tony.
If you wanna say something, just get it out.

TONY. I ain't got nothing to say.

EVELYN. Then stop acting like you got something on your mind.

TONY. Ain't nothing on my mind.

EVELYN. Good.
Mine neither.

TONY. Alright.

EVELYN. Alright.

> *Beat.*

TONY. You expecting.
You lost your senses a little bit.
It never happened.

EVELYN. It never happened.

TONY. Never happened.

> *Beat.*

EVELYN. I am sorry.

TONY. You ain't got nothing to apologize for.

EVELYN. To Sally.
She didn't deserve that.
And for making you out like my no-good daddy,
you didn't deserve that either.

TONY. You ain't sorry for saying Bowzie dead?

EVELYN. No.

TONY. You don't have nobody dead in your family, do you?

EVELYN. I lost a baby. That's all the loss I need in my life.

TONY. Well I lost my mama and my daddy.
Nine years old, moved to Dry Creek.
Didn't know a soul.
Maybe that's why I'm the only one hoping to hear from Bowzie.
'Cause I'm the only one know what it is to never hear a loved one's voice again.

EVELYN. I'd rather hear nothing than hear from the morgue.

> *Sally enters the house. Immediately, Tony moves his leg.*
> *She looks. She calculates.*

SALLY. Something wrong with your leg, Tony?

TONY. Evelyn just doing a little trick to get rid of chiggers.

SALLY. What you got chiggers for?

TONY. Messing around in the field at MacHenry's.

> *Sally heads for the fridge.*

SALLY. Uh huh.
Evelyn, you staying for dinner?

> *Evelyn looks to Tony.*

Oh, look at that.
You brought me some butterbeans?

TONY. Evelyn?

EVELYN. Yeah.
They had a sale.

> *Beat.*

SALLY. So, you two gonna tell me what's goin' on?

EVELYN. What do you mean, Sally?

SALLY. Tony, you gonna do the telling?

TONY. *(Standing.)* Sally…
Evelyn was beside herself the other week and got a little mixed up.

SALLY. A little mixed up.

EVELYN. I kissed him.

> *Beat.*

SALLY. She put her lips on you?

TONY. She was crying about Bowzie. Grieving.

SALLY. Mm.

EVELYN. It didn't mean nothing. I don't have no feelings for him, Sally. You know that.

SALLY. *(Coldly, to Tony.)* I know you don't want him, girl.
I hardly want him half the time, myself.

TONY. Sally.

SALLY. *(To Tony.)* Was you gonna tell me?

EVELYN. I was gonna—

SALLY. Tony. Was you gonna tell me? You don't think enough of me to tell me yourself?

EVELYN. Sally, it was really my—

SALLY. Tony?

> *Tony is silent.*

I guess don't nobody think too much of me anymore, do they?

> *Tony is silent.*

I reckon not.

> *Sally calmly re-pins her hat to her hair, snatches the keys, and walks out.*
>
> *The Pretty Green Chevy revs up and drives off.*

EVELYN. Why didn't you say nothing?

TONY. Say what?

EVELYN. Explain yourself. Tell her what it was.

TONY. Ain't nothing to say… I made a promise and I broke it.

EVELYN. You didn't break nothing. I'm the one—

TONY. You think I don't know that?
Goddamn Bowzie.
I'm trying to be the man of two houses, raise two babies, and what I get?
This.

EVELYN. I don't need your help, man.
I can take care of myself!
TONY. Then get the hell out, then!!!
You got a house.
Let me fix mine in peace.

> *Evelyn grabs her things and exits.*

10

> *Tony in his home.*
> *Evelyn searching for Sally.*
> *Sally downtown at a clothing store.*
> *Bowzie in a jail cell.*
> *Each of them are alone and separated by so many miles.*

11

> *Sally and Evelyn standing in the field. There is no warmth between them.*

SALLY. Thank you for holding my pocketbook.
EVELYN. You're welcome.

> *Silence.*

You know, Sally…

> *She trails off.*

I knew you would be downtown.
I know you ride those escalators when you need cheering up.
SALLY. Harvey's knew what they were doing when they got them.
EVELYN. *(An attempt at levity.)* Entertainment free of charge.

> *Sally does not laugh.*

I know I shouldn't've tracked you down like that, but I was worried—
SALLY. I…

EVELYN. Just say it. Get it out.

SALLY. While I was looking at those pretty clothes,
and picking out what dresses I might find the sewing patterns to…
I did something I never done before.
Ever.
For the first time in my life, I wondered…
You know, it never crossed my mind 'til tonight.
She was sitting right on my bladder, and I had to tinkle something
awful.
I passed all those clothes.
I passed the restroom.
I passed the diner counters.
I walked out of the store.
I walked all the way down Church Street to the alley.
To that box.
And I handed you my purse…

EVELYN. I didn't mind it, Sally.

SALLY. You shouldn't have to.
Pregnant or not,
nobody ought to hold nobody's pocketbook so they can use the
bathroom shopping.

EVELYN. I am so sorry—

SALLY. I wish there was a Freedom Ride for those boxes.
They hopping on air-conditioned buses
complaining about where they get to sit
when my daughter might have to watch her mama squat like a dog
over a box 'cause ain't no Colored restrooms on Church Street.
Like a dog.
Without an ounce of dignity.
…That's exactly what it was.
I'm squatting while you hold my pocketbook.
I…hate that.

> *"Hate" is on her list of dirty words.*

You go out in the world all day. Everybody treat you like a dog out
there.
And you come to your own house and get treat like a dog there.

69

Then you invite somebody in your home—your sister—
and get treat like a dog.
Everywhere.
I want a…
I want a *god damn* Freedom Ride for me, Evelyn.
Where's my god damn freedom?

   Evelyn doesn't respond.

(Nearly to tears.) I'm asking you.
I need to know.
Where?

EVELYN. I can't tell you that, Sally.
I don't even know for myself.
I wish I did…

  A long,   *long beat.*

SALLY. Do you remember how we met?

EVELYN. Of course.

SALLY. Well?

EVELYN. You were working at the delicatessen
and your coworker, James…James—

SALLY. James Cunningham.

EVELYN. Cunningham.
Flirted with me every time I came in—Sally, you sure you want to—

SALLY. Keep going.

EVELYN. I need you to understand that—

SALLY. Keep going.

EVELYN. One day he asked me outright.
Would I go down with him to the arcade[12] that evening.
You was standing right there. Quiet as always.

SALLY. And what'd you say next?

EVELYN. I said I only go on double dates. And I asked him who's
gonna take *you*.
He said you already had you a fella sweet on you.
And I say,

12 Pronounced "are-kay"

Well the three of y'all meet me there or he might as well keep his advances.

Low and behold, you and Tony came on.

SALLY. I didn't know you from Adam
but Tony said "To heck with it." And there we were.
You wearing that ol' bop-tail dress.
Every time you walk, just bopping your tail.

EVELYN. And you looking like a nun.
We had us a good old time.
We took pictures and got popcorn.
Took us two whole hours to walk from Fourth Avenue to Fifth
and when we got to the five and dime,

SALLY. *(Joining the recollection.)* —McClellen's.

EVELYN. McClellen's…had ice cream and hot dogs.
Never went out with that James again. But I knew you and Tony was my kind of folk.

SALLY. And we felt the same way about you…
It was Tony who got the notion to introduce you to Bowzie.
He told Bowzie to go on down to where you was singing—

EVELYN. I can't lose you, Sally.
I got a whole mess of siblings, and you the closest thing I got to a sister.
I can't lose you.

> *Beat.*

SALLY. I just gotta ask…

EVELYN. Anything!

SALLY. Was that why you wanted me to leave him?

EVELYN. God no, Sally. Jesus.

SALLY. Don't take His name in vain.

EVELYN. No.
No no no. A hundred times over.
It was a stupid, stupid mistake.
It was a mistake; I just lost myself.

SALLY. *(Cold as ice.)* "For if you forgive men when they sin against you,
your heavenly Father will also forgive you."

EVELYN. I am so, so sorry.

SALLY. I'm watching you, girl.

EVELYN. Watch me. As long as you don't quit me.

SALLY. With God's help…
Here. You should have these.

Sally hands her a bundle of envelopes.

EVELYN. What's this?

SALLY. Letters.

EVELYN. I can see that.
They're from Bowzie.
Addressed to you.
Why?

SALLY. He wrote me.

EVELYN. This one dates back to when he left.
You been talking to him the whole time?

SALLY. No. I never wrote back.
Didn't feel right.

EVELYN. But hiding letters did?

SALLY. He needed somebody to confide in.

EVELYN. Confide in?

SALLY. Talk to.

EVELYN. *(Reading.)* "Parchman Penitentiary"
He in jail?

SALLY. He kept trying to call you, but you wouldn't answer his calls.

EVELYN. *(Reading.)* "Don't tell Evelyn."

SALLY. *(Exiting.)* I'll leave you to them.

EVELYN. Sally.

SALLY. Yes?

EVELYN. Take them.

SALLY. Take 'em?

EVELYN. He wrote them to you.
Ain't none of my business.

SALLY. They about you.
Every single one of them.
He your husband.

EVELYN. No.
No, I don't think so.

SALLY. Evelyn—

      Evelyn rips the letters one by one.

Stop that.
Stop that!
Evelyn Brandon, you stop that right now.

EVELYN. There.
Now they're between you and him just like he wanted.

SALLY. Look what you've done.

EVELYN. He is dead to me.

SALLY. Girl, he's alive. He's not—

EVELYN. *(A cry for help.)* He.
Is.
Dead.
To.
Me.

SALLY. Oh, Evelyn.

EVELYN. Don't you quit me.

SALLY. Oh, Evelyn.

EVELYN. We're in this together.
Don't you quit me.

12

      Bowzie on the telephone.

BOWZIE. Come on, Evelyn.
Pick up.
Pick up.

TONY. Hello?

BOWZIE. Hello?

TONY. Bowzie?!

Bowzie is silent.

Bowzie? Is that you?

Bowzie nods.

Hello? You there?

BOWZIE. Yeah, it's me.

TONY. Niggah, it sure is good to hear your voice.

Bowzie is silent.

I'ma need you to speak to me, man.

BOWZIE. Evelyn alright?

TONY. She managing. How you?

BOWZIE. Not too hot, man. Not too hot.

TONY. What's going on? They ain't treating you right?

BOWZIE. I call my house and you pick up the telephone.

TONY. I'm here looking for Sally—

BOWZIE. Yeah.

TONY. Niggah, it's been over a month since anybody heard from you and you cross with me?

BOWZIE. Shit, man. What you want from me? I'm in jail—

TONY. Jail?

BOWZIE. —I ain't hear from my wife
and some niggah is answering my telephone?

TONY. So I'm some niggah now?

BOWZIE. Far as I can tell. Put my wife on the damn telephone.

TONY. Your wife ain't here.
And I don't care if you was locked up in the Pentagon,
you ain't talking to me like that.
Now cool it.

BOWZIE. Don't tell me to cool it, man! Don't you tell me to cool it!

TONY. Calm down.

BOWZIE. *(Booming.)* Goddammit, I am calm!

    A beat.

(Quieter.) I am calm.

    Tony is silent.

(Actually calm.) I'm calm...
I just...
this place ain't pretty.
And I don't know how I'm gonna get out.

TONY. ...How much you need?

BOWZIE. This is my mess—

TONY. You already ain't going to school.
Your wife pregnant and alone.
You need this money more than I do.
How much you need to get out of jail?

BOWZIE. She's what?

TONY. She ain't want to tell you, but she pregnant.
Not too far along, but you need to be here.

BOWZIE. Whose is it?

TONY. I'm just trying to help.
Don't think like that.

BOWZIE. You been helping, alright.

TONY. What's that supposed to mean?

BOWZIE. You know what the hell I mean.
Or you need me to spell it out?
Oh, that's right! That won't do no good—

TONY. Okay.
Okay, if I'm the punching bag you need.
Go ahead.
I'm open.
Hit me.

    Bowzie is silent.

Hit me!

    Bowzie is silent.

Niggah, throw your best punch.

Get it all out, 'cause next time you ain't gon' be so lucky.
You waste your call fussing at me when I'm trying to help you.
I've done my dirt, but—dammit—you gon' let me be a new man.
Everybody gon' let me be a new man!
You my family.
Evelyn and y'all's baby is my family.
How—much—do—you—need?
I'll work whatever I gotta work,
I'll give you all my savings,
but you need to be here. She need you *here*.
You done rode your little bus
and done your marching or whatever the hell you needed to do.
But you are not Martin
fucking
Luther King.
I'm sorry but you ain't.
You ain't nobody.
You don't belong there. You got too much to lose.
You can't afford bail and you can't afford schooling.
You threw it away, man.
It's our fault 'cause we let you. You too good for this world,
but you gon' get your ass out that prison and back here where you belong.
I got the money to help if you just use the good sense God gave you.
Your family need you. We need you!

BOWZIE. …They won't give us toothbrushes.
I can't remember the last time I brushed my teeth.
My mouth hurts. My stomach hurts.
My gums bleed whenever I bite into…
They give us food with bugs…sometimes they even drench it in salt
first.
The guards show off their shotguns
and leather whips.
They got mad we wouldn't stop singing.
So they took the mattresses.
I started sleeping on the floor because at night,
it gets real cold. And they turn on the fans so the bed is even colder.
Shoot, I always thought it never got cold in Mississippi. But nights?

Nights are something else when you naked with the fan on
and no mattress
and no sheets
and no food
and no toothbrush
and no—

TONY. Bowzie.

BOWZIE. *(Falling apart.)* Tony
They tease us. And some of the fellas.
They don't take too well to it.
And.
They use fire hoses to smash the troublemakers against the bars,
And they shout, "Y'all know we got a graveyard here, too!

TONY. Stop.

BOWZIE. *(Pulling himself together.)* But you know what?
If I never get to finish school.
If I never earn more than enough money to make it payday to
payday,
it'll all be worth it.
Because my son will ride a bus and sit wherever he wants to.
Not worrying if some men in sheets are gonna come put a bullet in
his body.
My daughter will be able to visit her grandparents with her girlfriends
and not worry about if the police are going to harass her!
And it'll be because their father
—me—
sacrificed everything he had
for just one more liberty.

TONY. Do you want to stay in jail
or do you want the money to get out?

BOWZIE. I would need all of the money you got saved.

TONY. Then that's what you're gonna get, brother.

> *Evelyn enters and sees Tony on the telephone. Tony makes eye
> contact.*

I just need to know if you still sacrificing
or if you ready to come home to your family?

BOWZIE. …I'm ready.

> *Evelyn gestures for the telephone.*
>
> *Tony hands it to her.*
>
> *Tony exits.*

I'm so ready.

I miss her so much.

EVELYN. Mmph.

BOWZIE. Evelyn?!

EVELYN. Mm hm.

BOWZIE. We're having another baby.

And you didn't tell me.

EVELYN. You been writing letters to Sally.

BOWZIE. You wouldn't pick up the telephone.

EVELYN. What you need to talk to *me* about?

BOWZIE. Some comfort.

Some conversation?

EVELYN. You didn't need no conversation when you left.

Why you need to talk now that you gone.

BOWZIE. How long you known you've been pregnant?

EVELYN. Couple months.

BOWZIE. …you should've told me.

EVELYN. If you wanna run off on me, don't let a child be the reason you stay.

Have me looking crazy like I don't know who my baby's father is.

I *know* who my child's father is.

BOWZIE. Stop being mean.

EVELYN. I'm not being—

BOWZIE. It's me, Evelyn.

Stop being mean for two seconds.

> *Evelyn breathes.*

(*Knowing her.*) Relax your eyebrows.

> *Evelyn does so.*

Take that air out your cheeks.

Evelyn does so.

I miss you, baby.

I miss how you wake up in the middle of the night just to fix the covers.

How you join in singing when I'm humming to myself and don't even realize it.

How your left eye blinks a little slower than your right one when you been drinking—

EVELYN. *(Swallowing a giggle.)* Hush your mouth.

BOWZIE. You hear me, baby?

EVELYN. You made a decision about us without me.

BOWZIE. It was *for* us.

EVELYN. For us, About us—either way, I didn't have no kind of say.
I'm having a baby. You decide where you wanna be.

BOWZIE. I want to be with you.

EVELYN. Then be with me.
And raise our child.

BOWZIE. I'm gonna come back.
Tony is going to bail me out with money he's been saving.
I already know what you're gonna say.
I promise we'll pay back every cent.

EVELYN. Alright, Jack.

BOWZIE. I'm not gonna go to school am I, baby?

EVELYN. Oh, you're gonna apply again.
And again. Until you get in.
You ain't gonna waste that brain you got.
Because I'm done.

BOWZIE. Done?

EVELYN. Yeah I'm done, Mr. Freedom Rider.
I'm gonna be a mother.
Hell, that's gonna be my Freedom Ride:
Raising a family.
Time for me to do what I want.
I'm gonna sit my ass down and put some work into *my* dreams.
The only audience I'ma be singing for

will be my six Baby Bowzies as their daddy's bringing home the bacon for once.

BOWZIE. *(Smiling.)* Sure 'nough?

EVELYN. Sure 'nough.

BOWZIE. My time on the telephone's almost up, Evelyn.

EVELYN. I'll be here.

BOWZIE. I did it for a reason.

EVELYN. We all got reasons for what we do.
As long as our hearts are in the right place.

BOWZIE. I love you, Evelyn Brandon.

EVELYN. …I love you too, Bowzie Brandon.

13

Tony enters his home.
There is a suitcase by the door.

TONY. *(Calling.)* Sally?!
Sally?!

Sally, dressed for bed, turns the light on.

Sally.
I been looking for you.

Sally doesn't respond.

I'm glad you're here.

SALLY. Just for tonight.
Daddy is picking me up first thing in the morning.

TONY. Baby, you don't have to—

SALLY. Tony, I'm going to bed.
Good night.

TONY. I got something I want to show you.
Can I show you first?
Then you can do whatever you want.

SALLY. Is it the box under the Frigidaire?

TONY. …you know about that?

SALLY. I found it while I was packing my things tonight.
Is that what you want to show me?

TONY. Yes.

SALLY. I don't want to see it.

TONY. I need you to see it.

SALLY. Well that don't got nothing to do with me.
What you need ain't got a thing to do with me.

TONY. *You* need to see it.

SALLY. I don't think I need anything from you, Tony.
I think today, I stopped needing anything—

TONY. She was *grieving*, Sally.
Grief so deep, you can't give it nothing but compassion.

SALLY. And since when you start giving that out?

TONY. Sally-Mae! I love you so hard.
I love you so hard my blood, my bones, my skin *ache* for you.
When you was yapping with Evelyn.
Reciting "He dead to me" like a Bible verse
—I felt it. I did.
I'm trying here.
I'm suffering.

SALLY. I am tired of suffering 'cause you suffering.
I am so tired, Tony.

TONY. …I don't make you happy no more?
How about our house?
Our marriage?
Our family?
What we done built?—

SALLY. This *house*, Tony?
This house?
This ain't where my battle supposed to be.
I'm supposed to be *home* here. I'm supposed to be *safe* here.

> *Tony listens.*

Tony takes it in.

Tony goes to his stash and opens it.

TONY. Look at this.

Look at it.

SALLY. I've seen it, Tony.

TONY. It's for a house, baby.

I ain't been riffin' and raffin'.

I ain't been gambling.

I been working extra and saving and scraping

and I put a payment down on a house.

I was going to, I mean.

I was gonna surprise you.

Have Bowzie move all our things while you was in the infirmary.

And then take our new family to our new home.

I been trying my hardest to keep the secret this whole time.

To surprise you.

Bowzie need the money for bail, so we gon' have to wait on the move

But this house will do.

This one right here.

You can be safe here.

You *are* safe here.

I love you.

Here.

> *He places the box in her hands.*

I love you.

And I am so sorry.

For everything.

I take full responsibility.

> *Sally looks to the money, then back at her husband.*

> *Sally tries but fails at finding the words to express herself.*

SALLY. …say that again?

TONY. I take full responsibility.

SALLY. *(Almost moved to tears.)* …one more time.

TONY. Baby. I'm wrong. I know I'm wrong—

SALLY. Just!

82

…just say what I asked you to.

TONY. I take full responsibility, baby.

SALLY. *(A realization.)* Thank you.

> *Sally begins to put her jacket on.*

TONY. Where you going, Sally?

SALLY. …thank you for taking responsibility.
And thank you for telling me your little secret.
Bowzie's lucky to have you.
I knew you were hiding something.
Thank you for finally deciding to tell me.
That's what respect looks like.

> *Sally walks out of the door.*
>
> *We stay with Tony for a moment as he places the box on top of the refrigerator.*
>
> *He looks out of the screen door, alone. Sally is gone. And all he wants is for her to come to bed where she belongs.*

14

> *Lights up slowly on Sally in the middle of an open field; there is a light drizzle.*
>
> *Her eyes are watering, her nightgown is muddy, and her belly is so full.*
>
> *She is a flower.*
>
> *She falls to her knees.*
>
> *She digs her hands into the mud.*
>
> *She breathes hard. Huh!*
>
> *And again. Huh!*

SALLY. Dear Bowzie,

Thank you for writing me.
I know it's ill-timed that I'm writing you just as you're getting out.
There are things you should know.

Before you get back.

I went to church the other night. Wednesday night Bible study.
They let Mother Cassandra Becton lead because she said she had a
Word on her heart and the Lord had told her that it was for some-
body in the building.
Her Word brought tears to my eyes,
but I do believe that Word is for you.

She say when each of her boys came of age, she take 'em to Old
Hickory Lake.
Then say, "Pick a rock."
And none of them know why, but she just tell 'em, "Pick a rock, boy."
And they did.
And she say, "That's your rock.
You put it in your pocket and take it with you everywhere you go.
Don't never let it loose.
Never.
And whenever you mad you stepped in a puddle
or whenever something don't go your way,
you grab that stone and thank God.
Think of one thing to be grateful for.
Because no matter if the whole world turn its back on you
and don't nothing go your way,
there's always *something* to be grateful for."

Bowzie, sometime it don't look like there's much at all to be grateful
for, I know.

I know,

I know,
I truly know.

Sometime that rock get so heavy in your pocket
'cause you can't figure out what to be grateful for.

Sometime it get so heavy.

It's so heavy.

> *She raises to one knee.*

It's so heavy.

She stands with great effort.

But pick it up.

> *She looks to her house.*
>
> *She looks to Bowzie's ripped letters.*

Pick it up anyhow.

Hold it 'til you figure it out.

> *She steels herself.*
>
> *She holds her stomach.*
>
> *Evelyn holds her own stomach.*
>
> *Bowzie holds his Fisk acceptance letter.*
>
> *Tony holds a bundle of money.*

We will figure it out...

> *With her final words,*
> *Sally holds her womb tight.*
>
> *Courage is a necessity.*
>
> *Change is unavoidable.*
>
> *Birth is labor.*
>
> *They all breathe hard,*
> *half-prayer, half-declaration: HUH!*

End of Play

PROPERTY LIST

(Use this space to create props lists for your production)

SOUND EFFECTS

(Use this space to create sound effects lists for your production)

Note on Songs/Recordings, Images, or Other Production Design Elements

The rights to perform "Evelyn's Song" are included with written performance licenses for this play. Please see your license for the sheet music and billing requirements.

Be advised that Dramatists Play Service neither holds the rights to nor grants permission to use any songs, recordings, images, or design elements mentioned in the play, other than the aforementioned "Evelyn's Song." It is the responsibility of the producing theater/organization to obtain permission of the copyright owner(s) for any such use. Additional royalty fees may apply for the right to use copyrighted materials.

For any songs/recordings, images, or other design elements mentioned in the play except for "Evelyn's Song," works in the public domain may be substituted. It is the producing theater/organization's responsibility to ensure the substituted work is indeed in the public domain. Dramatists Play Service cannot advise as to whether or not a song/arrangement/recording, image, or other design element is in the public domain.

the
HARD
SELTZER
cocktail book

the HARD SELTZER cocktail book

55 (UNOFFICIAL) Recipes
for White Claw® Slushies, Truly® Mixers, and More Spiked-Seltzer Drinks

Casie Vogel

Published in the US by:
Ulysses Press
PO Box 3440
Berkeley, CA 94703
www.ulyssespress.com

ISBN: 978-1-64604-185-5
Library of Congress Control Number: 2021930799

Printed in China
10 9 8 7 6 5 4 3 2 1

Managing editor: Claire Chun
Editor: Anne Healey
Proofreader: Renee Rutledge
Front cover design: David Hastings
Cover artwork: blue background © Magenta10/shutterstock.com; drinks
   © VECTOR FUN/shutterstock.com
Interior artwork: shutterstock.com except pages 29, 55, 79, 83, 91, 111
   © Michael Calcagno

To Michael

Contents

CHAPTER THREE: CLASSY CLASSICS 81

CHAPTER FOUR: PREGAME & PARTY 115

Introduction

Nothing sounds sweeter than the crack of that slim aluminum can, home to a 100-calorie bubbly beauty. Spring, summer, whatever the time of year, it's hard seltzer season.

At 4 to 6 percent alcohol content, it's not a bad deal! But sometimes you have to take it up a notch...or several. I mean, that's what we're all here for if we're being honest, right? Hard seltzer (also called spiked seltzer) is the perfect mixer to make a boozy drink that much boozier.

What's the right ratio? What actually tastes like a cocktail, doesn't skimp, but also doesn't immediately send you to blackout town? Well, my friend, that is where my help comes in. The recipes from here on out are dangerously delicious and designed to get the party going, whether it's a Friday night pregame or your next big party—or if it's just been a tough day (girl, you do you). Instead of that next round of probably (always) regrettable tequila shots, pick up this book and let's get bubbly.

WHAT IS HARD SELTZER, ANYWAY?

You may have noticed in stores that hard seltzer is in the refrigerated display case with all the beer. But it's not exactly beer, is it? The production process is very similar to beer, but seltzer is made from fermented cane sugar instead of malted barley. Most seltzers are advertised as being made with "real fruit juice," which is true (at least for the major brands)! That's where the flavor comes from—not from artificial sweeteners. As a result, we get to enjoy drinks that are low in calories and low in sugar. As an added bonus, most seltzers are gluten-free as well!

TYPES OF HARD SELTZER

As of this writing, there are a ton of different seltzer brands. Wherever you're reading this from, you have no doubt encountered the major players, such as White Claw, Truly, and Spiked Seltzer; but there are also tons of local booze players trying to get into this game. My scientific research[1] has shown that for the most part the seltzer flavors listed here often overlap between brands. In this book I've tried to use an assortment of the readily available flavors, so you should be able to find them at most stores. If you're having trouble, you can and should definitely trust your taste buds in terms of substitutions. Here's my advice on improvising with the various seltzer flavors:

Citrus flavors. When it comes to the "classics," citrus flavors—like lemon, orange, tangerine, clementine, grapefruit, and lime—are a must-have and are the easiest to swap out. Lime is by far the strongest of the citrus flavors; I personally feel it has a little more kick. When replacing, make sure to taste test.

---

1 Just kidding; do not mistake the author for someone who has any knowledge of science.

the **HARD SELTZER** *cocktail book*

Berry flavors. Berry flavors include strawberry, raspberry, cranberry, and mixed berry; they are pretty strong, so I wouldn't recommend mixing them with a dark liquor. They are great for upgrading your basic drinks without adding flavored syrup. For example, upgrading a classic lime daiquiri to raspberry would just require swapping out lime (or any other flavor) seltzer for raspberry seltzer!

Black cherry. You're either a black cherry person or you're not. If you are, you're in luck because the superstrong flavor profile will overpower most drinks. If you're looking to mask a ton of liquor, even tequila, black cherry is your new BFF. I don't include black cherry as a suggestion in many of these recipes because it is so overpowering. But if you really love it, feel free to swap it in.

"Tropical" flavors. Choices like passionfruit, pineapple, mango, and strawberry kiwi really shine in the frozen/slushy drinks, but feel free to mix and match.

Seasonal flavors. As of this writing, many of the major brands have come out with "seasonal" flavors that may or may not be available depending on when you're making these drinks. For example, in fall 2020, Bud Light debuted the Ugly Sweater variety pack, which included fall/winter-themed flavors like Apple Crisp and Ginger Snap. For the seasonal drinks, I've noted where you could give such seltzers a try. I've only suggested seasonal flavors for the holiday drinks and have offered substitutions if you don't have them on hand.

Sparkling hard cider. Many cideries are also making hard seltzer, or "sparkling" cider. Those are more apple-flavored than many of the traditional spiked seltzer flavors, but they work great in sangrias and tropical drinks. While sparkling cider is not technically a hard seltzer, I'm open to the substitution if you have it on hand!

Hard lemonade. Some of our go-to brands, such as Truly, have lemonade flavors that are particularly nice in the frozen cocktails. But brands like Mike's Hard Lemonade have been around forever and are essentially the same thing. You can absolutely use those as well!

> Trust your taste buds and use the flavors that you like. If you don't like pineapple, swap it out for another flavor. If you're not sure how to choose a substitution, just use a flavor you do like from the same variety pack. The other flavors that come in the box are often good choices.

OTHER BOOZE TO HAVE ON HAND

The recipes in this book range from classic martinis to jungle juice. If you want to make them all, you may need to start stocking your bar. Classic liquors are always good to have around, but make sure to check recipes for some of the more out-there punches, which use some less common liquors and liqueurs!

THE CLASSICS

While there are plenty more liquors out there that you can have on your bar cart, the necessary ones for this book are listed below. Believe it or not, it's not just clear liquors on this list!

- ✦ Bourbon
- ✦ Brandy
- ✦ Cognac
- ✦ Cointreau or triple sec
- ✦ Gin
- ✦ Rum (dark and light)
- ✦ Rye
- ✦ Tequila (the blanco, or silver, variety)
- ✦ Vermouth (dry and sweet varieties)
- ✦ Vodka

WINE

I hope that this is obvious, but don't go using that bottle of wine you've been saving since your trip to Paris for the recipes in this book. Use wines that you like, but certainly don't spend more than $20 on a bottle. Here are some suggested wines to have around:

- ✦ Prosecco or other sparkling white wine
- ✦ Red wine, ideally Spanish for sangria
- ✦ Rosé
- ✦ White wine

LESS COMMON LIQUEURS

You don't need to go crazy here, but you may need some less common liqueurs to round out these drinks. It's always smart to have a bottle (or two) of Aperol at the ready—every party loves a spritz!

* Aperol (a bitter, bright orange Italian apéritif)

* Blue curaçao (a bright blue liqueur from Curaçao that's flavored with laraha, a native bitter orange)

* Campari (a bitter, dark red Italian apéritif)

* Coconut-flavored rum (such as Malibu)

* Peach schnapps

MIXERS, GARNISHES, AND OTHER ACCOUTREMENTS

It's not just about the booze! You'll need some nonalcoholic additions to make your cocktails complete. This list has everything, from your classic mixers (like orange juice and cranberry juice cocktail) to the unexpected (like soy sauce and vanilla ice cream).

MIXERS

There's a lot of juice on this list of mixers. If you can find it (or squeeze it), fresh juice is always preferable.

- Apple cider or juice
- Bitters (such as Angostura or Peychaud's)
- Black tea
- Cola soft drink
- Cranberry juice cocktail
- Cream of coconut
- Fruit punch
- Ginger beer
- Grapefruit juice
- Grenadine
- Lemon juice
- Lemonade
- Lime juice
- Orange juice
- Peach or apricot puree/nectar
- Pineapple juice
- Simple syrup
- Soda water
- Tomato juice or Clamato

Easy Simple Syrup

There's no reason to buy simple syrup—it's supereasy to make it yourself. I like to have some available at all times. You never know when you want a cocktail ASAP! Make some now and keep it handy.

The ratio is 1:1; you can scale this up or down as needed. Store the syrup in the fridge, and it should keep for about four weeks.

> 1 cup white sugar
> 1 cup water

1. Combine the sugar and water in a small saucepan over medium heat.

2. Stir until the sugar is dissolved. Remove from the heat and let cool completely.

3. Pour the syrup into an airtight glass container (I like to use a mason jar), and store it in the fridge.

OTHER ITEMS USED IN THESE RECIPES

You can keep these around for non-booze-related activities, too. Odds are you have most of them in your pantry or fridge already!

- Hot sauce
- Jell-O/gelatin
- Milk
- Soy sauce
- Vanilla extract
- Vanilla or raspberry ice cream
- Worcestershire sauce

FRESH/FROZEN FRUITS AND VEGETABLES

Frozen fruit is great for frozen drinks because it cuts down on how much ice you need to have on hand. If you don't like a particular fruit or are allergic, just swap it out for another you prefer instead.

- Cranberries, fresh
- Cucumber
- Grapefruit
- Green apple
- Lemon
- Lime
- Mango chunks, frozen
- Mixed berries, frozen and fresh
- Orange
- Seedless watermelon, fresh
- Strawberries, frozen and fresh

GARNISHES

Are garnishes absolutely necessary? No. Are they classy AF? You bet. Adding a fresh rosemary sprig or cinnamon stick to your cocktail can be the perfect touch for your Instagram story.

- ✦ Celery
- ✦ Celery salt
- ✦ Chili powder
- ✦ Cinnamon
- ✦ Egg whites
- ✦ Maraschino cherries
- ✦ Mint, fresh
- ✦ Nutmeg, ground
- ✦ Olives
- ✦ Paprika
- ✦ Pepper
- ✦ Rosemary, fresh
- ✦ Sea salt
- ✦ Sugar
- ✦ Sugar cubes

TOOLS YOU'LL NEED

You don't need to buy a fancy bartender's kit for these recipes, but you will need a few crucial supplies. If you're packing items for a bachelorette weekend or just want to make sure your kitchen is outfitted, here are the essentials:

Bar spoon. This is really just a long spoon for mixing cocktails that aren't shaken. If you don't have a bar spoon, you can substitute with the longest spoon in your kitchen.

Blender. Any stationary blender will work for frozen cocktails.

Cocktail shaker. Also known as a "cobbler shaker," the classic cocktail shaker consists of a cup, strainer, and lid, perfect for shaking, mixing, and pouring.

Ice pop molds and wooden sticks. These are only used for the Clawsicles (page 65). Not all ice pop molds require wooden sticks, so check what kind of molds you have.

Juicer. I highly recommend using fresh juice whenever you can. A small manual juicer is great to have; mine fits on top of a mason jar and doesn't take up too much room in my drawers.

Large pitcher or punch bowl. Select a pitcher or punch bowl that can hold at least a gallon; you'll want to make sure that you have enough to go around for the party drinks.

Measuring cups. When it comes to large-batch cocktails, you'll put away the shot glass and start working with larger quantities, so you will need measuring cups in three sizes: ¼ cup, ½ cup, and 1 cup.

Paring knife and small cutting board. A small knife and cutting board will be nice to have for slicing lime wedges and other garnishes.

Plastic condiment cups. These are only used for the Sparkling Jell-O Shots (page 120). Usually 2 ounces, these often come with plastic lids that are great for storing in the fridge.

Shot glass. A shot glass is a must-have. Most are 1 or 2 ounces; make sure you know what size you have so you don't under- or over-pour. This is used for measuring, so if you're buying a new shot glass, I recommend getting one with fill lines that show the amounts on the side.

SELTZER-FRIENDLY GLASSWARE

I've offered suggestions for glassware where appropriate, but honestly, these are some pretty hefty cocktails. Unfortunately, all those cute coupes and dainty champagne glasses are out of the picture unless you're serving from a pitcher. I've downsized this glassware list to the major oversized glassware (and some more creative variations) that can hold anywhere from 8 to 16 ounces of liquid. Feel free to pick and choose when you're crafting these recipes!

Oversized cocktail glasses. You probably know the cocktail glass as a martini glass. Most martini glasses that you buy at the store these days are technically "oversized"; make sure yours are properly huge (more than 10-ounce capacity).

Double old-fashioned glasses. Also known as a rocks glass. Make sure you've got doubles—these cocktails are certainly not singles.

Wine glasses. Don't try to break out those tiny free glasses you got at a wine tasting; you are going to need the big mamas for these cocktails. I recommend using white-wine glasses over red because they're designed to keep drinks cooler for longer.

Margarita glasses. These shallow-bowled, wide-rimmed glasses aren't just for margs! Feel free to break these out for any of the frozen cocktails.

Hurricane glasses. Nothing screams "hot summer days" like the curves of a hurricane glass.

Copper mugs. This one is traditionally used to serve a Moscow mule, but it's great for these cocktails if you want to keep things cool and classy.

Pint glasses. Your classic beer glass is perfect for these cocktails. It's got the capacity to handle ice, seltzer, and liquor.

Highball glasses. Tall and skinny, these glasses work well for all types of cocktails and are sure to impress in a pinch. A Collins glass is similar and works well also; the only difference is that it's slightly taller.

Mason jars. Not a traditional cocktail glass by any means, but it's a great (and cheap) way to keep it classy, serve a crowd, and still contain all that fizzy goodness.

Solo cups. I had to add it. Your trusty red plastic Solo cup absolutely does the trick here. It's certainly less classy, but no one said that you couldn't have a martini in a red cup.

A NOTE ON RECIPES AND ORGANIZATION

The recipes are organized into four different chapters based on the potential party you're hosting or the day-drinking situation you've found yourself in. For example, Chapter One, "Boozy Brunch," is full of your late-morning favorites, from mimosas to micheladas. If you're looking for a specific drink, you can always flip to the index.

With the exception of a few single-serving cocktails and the batch "party" cocktails, most of the recipes in this book use one 12-ounce can of hard seltzer and serve two. Feel free to scale up or down as needed.

Boozy Brunch

All hail, the queen of all meals: brunch.

No one is immune to her charms. I mean, who doesn't love brunch? Whether it's a bottomless deal or just the promise of day drinking with friends, a bubbly drink with your first meal of the day is the perfect weekend treat.

And hard seltzer is a crowning addition to a brunch cocktail. It pairs perfectly with icons like the Aperol spritz, Bellini, and mimosa and adds an interesting twist to savory girls like the Bloody Mary.

Whether you're enjoying brunch at home with the girls or looking to keep brunch vibes going well after your two-hour limit is up, this chapter has you covered.

Mega Mimosa

The brunch classic...but with a lot more booze. I like my mimosa to be light on the orange juice—with just enough to provide a bit of color. Add or subtract orange juice depending on how you like yours.

MAKES 2 DRINKS

6 ounces prosecco or sparkling white wine

1 (12-ounce) can orange hard seltzer

orange juice, to taste

✦ Split the prosecco and the seltzer between two glasses.

✦ Top with the orange juice to taste.

> Any citrus-flavor hard seltzer will work great here! I highly recommend trying it out with grapefruit, pineapple, or mango. This recipe can also be doubled, tripled, or quadrupled depending on the size of your brunch party.

Boozier Bellini

Bellinis aren't typically served over ice, but since these are rather large drinks, I recommend throwing in a few cubes to keep things cool as you sip. Orange or tangerine hard seltzer is a good alternative here if you don't have mango on hand.

MAKES 2 DRINKS

4 ounces peach or apricot puree/nectar

6 ounces prosecco or other sparkling white wine

1 (12-ounce) can mango hard seltzer

peach slices, for garnish

✦ Fill two glasses with ice. Split the peach or apricot puree between the glasses.

✦ Top each glass with 3 ounces of prosecco followed by half a can (6 ounces) of seltzer.

✦ Drop in the peach slices and serve.

> Quadruple this recipe if you want to use an entire bottle of sparkling wine.

Aperol Spritz-o-Clock

This classic Italian apéritif isn't just good before a meal—it's always spritz-o-clock in my book. You can use soda water instead of the prosecco, but it's much more fun to triple down on the alcohol.

MAKES 2 DRINKS

6 ounces Aperol

4 ounces prosecco or soda water

1 (12-ounce) can orange hard seltzer

orange wedges, for garnish

✦ Fill two glasses with ice. Split the Aperol between the glasses (3 ounces each).

✦ Split the prosecco or soda water between the glasses (2 ounces each).

✦ Top each glass with half a can (6 ounces) of seltzer. Garnish each glass with an orange wedge.

Spritzy Screwdriver

The screwdriver is a dangerously delicious brunch choice; imbibe carefully. For this one, try out some different hard seltzer flavors, such as mango, pineapple, or grapefruit.

MAKES 2 DRINKS

3 ounces vodka

6 ounces orange juice

1 (12-ounce) can orange hard seltzer

orange wedges, for garnish

✦ Fill two glasses with ice. Add 1½ ounces of vodka to each glass.

✦ Split the orange juice between the two glasses (3 ounces each).

✦ Top each glass with half a can (6 ounces) of seltzer. Garnish each with an orange wedge.

Fizzy Fuzzy Navel

Make brunch totally rad with this classic '80s cocktail. This twist brings it into the 2020s by adding some bodacious bubbles.

MAKES 2 DRINKS

¼ cup peach schnapps

¼ cup orange juice

1 (12-ounce) can orange hard seltzer

orange wedges, for garnish

✦ Fill a cocktail shaker with ice. Add the peach schnapps and the orange juice. Stir.

✦ Strain into two glasses filled with ice.

✦ Top each glass with half a can (6 ounces) of seltzer. Garnish each with an orange wedge.

> Try this one with pineapple or mango seltzer!

Lazy Gal's Greyhound

Grapefruit is my go-to hard seltzer flavor. I've been known to spike it more than once with a little vodka and make what I call a "Lazy Gal's Greyhound." It's definitely better with grapefruit juice, but I've marked it as optional in the event that you are just looking to keep it fast and loose.

MAKES 1 DRINK

1 ounce vodka

1 (12-ounce) can grapefruit hard seltzer

1–2 ounces grapefruit juice, to taste (optional)

✦ Fill a pint glass with ice and add all the ingredients. Stir gently (this will be a full glass!)

Bubbly Mary

Don't repeat this one too many times. Not that you'll summon Bloody Mary—but you may summon a hangover. I like lemon hard seltzer for this recipe, but feel free to try it with lime!

MAKES 1 DRINK

SALT RIM
1 teaspoon
celery salt

1 teaspoon
black pepper

1 teaspoon
smoked paprika

✦ Combine the salt rim ingredients in a small bowl. Pour onto a small plate.

✦ Rub the lemon wedge around the rim of a glass to moisten it. Place the juiced rim on the plate with the salt rim mix, pressing gently to coat it. Fill the glass with ice.

BUBBLY MARY

1 lemon wedge

1 ounce vodka

3 ounces tomato
juice or Clamato

1 dash
Worcestershire sauce

2 dashes hot sauce
(such as Tabasco)

1 tablespoon
lime juice

1 tablespoon
lemon juice

½ (12-ounce) can
lemon hard seltzer
(approximately
6 ounces)

celery, olives,
cornichons, shrimp,
and/or bacon,
for garnish

✦ Fill a cocktail shaker with ice. Add all
the ingredients except the garnishes.

✦ Shake a few times to combine. Don't
overshake—you don't want to shake all
the bubbles out of the seltzer.

✦ Strain into the prepared glass. Add any
desired garnishes.

Más Michelada

Find your beach without the beer. Lime hard seltzer is the perfect substitute.

MAKES 1 DRINK

SPICE MIX
1 teaspoon chili powder

½ teaspoon coarse sea salt

MICHELADA
1 lime wedge

1 dash Worcestershire sauce

1 dash soy sauce

1 dash hot sauce (such as Tabasco)

1 ounce lime juice

3 ounces tomato juice or Clamato

1 (12-ounce) can lime hard seltzer

lime wheel, for garnish (optional)

✦ Combine the chili powder and the sea salt in a small bowl. Spread onto a small plate.

✦ Rub the lime wedge around the rim of a glass to moisten it. Place the moistened rim onto the plate with the spice mix, pressing gently to coat it.

✦ Fill the glass with ice. Add a pinch of the spice mix to the glass.

✦ Add all the remaining ingredients except the garnish. Gently stir to mix. Garnish with the lime wedge or lime wheel.

One-Minute Margarita (On the Rocks)

Check out page 77 for a big-batch frozen margarita recipe, but if you're looking for a quick on-the-rocks version, you're in the right place.

MAKES 2 DRINKS

1 lime wedge, to rim glass (optional)

sea salt, to rim glass (optional)

3 ounces blanco tequila

1 ounce Cointreau

2 ounces lime juice

1 (12-ounce) can lime hard seltzer

lime wheels, for garnish

✦ If a salt rim is desired, rub the lime wedge around the rims of two glasses to moisten. Dip the rims in the sea salt to coat.

✦ Fill the glasses with ice.

✦ Fill a cocktail shaker with ice. Add the tequila, Cointreau, lime juice, and seltzer. Shake until chilled.

✦ Strain into the glasses. Garnish each with a lime wheel.

You can play around with seltzer flavors on this one. Strawberry and raspberry are great ways to make this go from the classic lime margarita to a flavored margarita without added fruit or syrup.

Tequila Sunrise to Sunset

Since brunch never happens at sunrise, this is a nice consolation prize. Of course, if you do this right, brunch might last until sunset!

MAKES 2 DRINKS

4 ounces blanco tequila

8 ounces orange juice

1 (12-ounce) can orange hard seltzer

2 teaspoons grenadine

maraschino cherries, for garnish

orange wheels, for garnish

✦ Fill two glasses with ice. Split the tequila, orange juice, and seltzer between them. Stir until mixed.

✦ Add 1 teaspoon of the grenadine to each glass, allowing it to sink to the bottom.

✦ Garnish each glass with a maraschino cherry and an orange wheel.

Although the recipe calls for orange seltzer, any of the tropical-flavor seltzers will work here! Pineapple is a nice spin. It's tempting to use black cherry seltzer in place of the grenadine here, but I feel it doesn't give the drink that same flavor. Plus, you don't get the red sunrise look without the grenadine.

Dealer's Choice White Sangria

In this recipe, hard seltzer stands in for the flavored liquor that's usually found in sangria. This is a true dealer's choice—pick any of your favorite hard seltzer flavors. I suggest grapefruit or strawberry! Feel free to mix up the fruit to match whatever seltzer you choose.

MAKES 4–6 DRINKS

1 (750-milliliter) bottle white wine, chilled

1 cup strawberries, halved

1 large orange, sliced

1 large green apple, cubed

2 ounces simple syrup (optional)

1–2 (12-ounce) cans hard seltzer (any flavor), to taste

✦ Combine all the ingredients in a pitcher. Serve over ice.

✦ If making ahead, combine all the ingredients except the seltzer, and store in the fridge. Just before serving, add the seltzer to the pitcher and stir, then pour into glasses. This maximizes bubbles!

Dealer's Choice Red Sangria

Another dealer's choice when it comes to your choice of hard seltzer flavor. For red sangria, I suggest going with a citrus flavor, like lemon, lime, orange, or grapefruit.

**MAKES
4–6 DRINKS**

1 (750-milliliter) bottle red wine, ideally Spanish

1 large orange, sliced

1 lemon, sliced

1 large green apple, cubed

2 ounces simple syrup (optional)

1–2 (12-ounce) cans hard seltzer (any flavor), to taste

✦ Combine all the ingredients in a pitcher. Serve over ice.

✦ If making ahead, combine all the ingredients except the seltzer, and store in the fridge. Just before serving, add the seltzer to the pitcher and stir, then pour. This maximizes bubbles!

Mom's White Wine Spritzer

The wine spritzer isn't just for moms. True day drinkers know that this drink is actually the ultimate brunch power move. It's the best way to guarantee a buzz that lasts for hours. With this spiked seltzer combo, you'll have to admit, your mom was right about this one.

MAKES 1 DRINK

3 ounces white wine, chilled

½ (12-ounce) can lime hard seltzer, chilled (approximately 6 ounces)

lime wheel, for garnish

✦ Fill a large wine glass with ice (this is optional; if all the ingredients are very, very cold you can skip the ice).

✦ Add the wine. Top with the seltzer.

✦ Garnish with the lime wheel.

> If you'd like to scale up or down, the ratio here is 1 part wine, 2 parts seltzer.

CHAPTER TWO

Summer Slushies

How to describe spiked seltzer on a hot summer day? Talented, brilliant, incredible, amazing, show-stopping, spectacular, never the same, completely not ever been done before, unafraid to reference or not reference, put it in a blender.[2]

Actually, blending hard seltzer into frozen cocktails has definitely been done before by many on social media. This chapter is packed with some classic frozen beverages, such as your margarita or daiquiri, but there are also some fun surprises, like the Boozy Berry Smoothie (page 57), inspired by the Costco food court, and Clawsicles (page 65). You heard me. Clawsicles.

Changing up flavors for any of these recipes is encouraged unless otherwise noted.

---

2 Attributed to Lady Gaga, aka Mother Monster. Not in reference to seltzer, but you get the idea.

Sparkling Frosé

A summertime stunner, frosé will steal the show at any poolside soiree. It requires some forethought, because you have to freeze the rosé the night before. That's the only way you can achieve that really perfect slushy texture. Trust me—it's worth it.

**MAKES
4–6 DRINKS**

1 (750-milliliter) bottle rosé wine

1 cup strawberries, frozen

1–2 ounces simple syrup, to taste

1 (12-ounce) can grapefruit hard seltzer

✦ Pour the wine into a gallon-size zip-lock bag. Freeze overnight.

✦ The next day add the strawberries, frozen rosé, and simple syrup to a blender. Blend until smooth.

✦ Add the seltzer and pulse a few times to mix.

✦ Serve immediately.

Watermelon Sugar Slushy

🍋 🍋 🍋

This watermelon slushy is dangerously refreshing—perfect for a hot day at the beach. Or for pretending that it's a hot day at the beach. In Malibu. With Harry Styles. Okay, too hot! Freeze the watermelon overnight; it is best served as cold as possible.

**MAKES
4–6 DRINKS**

4 cups seedless watermelon, chopped

1 cup vodka

2 ounces lime juice

1–2 ounces simple syrup, to taste

1 (12-ounce) can watermelon or lime hard seltzer

1 lime wedge, to rim glasses (optional)

sugar, to rim glasses (optional)

lime wheels, for garnish

✦ Put the watermelon in a large ziplock bag. Place in the freezer for a minimum of 1 hour, but ideally overnight.

✦ The next day, put the watermelon, vodka, lime juice, and simple syrup in a blender. Puree until the watermelon is completely liquefied.

✦ Add the seltzer and pulse a few times. You don't want to blend out all the bubbles, but you want this well mixed.

✦ If desired, rub a lime wedge around the rims of two large glasses. Dip in sugar.

✦ Pour into prepared glasses and garnish with lime wedges.

Boozy Berry Smoothie

Inspired by Costco's iconic mixed berry smoothie (we are high class here), this boozy concoction is perfect for that bag of bulk frozen berries. Feel free to use any berry hard seltzer here.

**MAKES
4-6 DRINKS**

¼ cup vodka

3-4 cups frozen mixed berries

1-2 ounces simple syrup, to taste

1-2 (12-ounce) cans berry hard seltzer, to taste

✦ Add the vodka, berries, and simple syrup to a blender. Blend until smooth.

✦ Add the first can of seltzer. Pulse until combined. Depending on desired consistency, add the second can.

✦ Serve immediately.

NSFW Frozen Lemonade

This sparkling frozen lemonade is a great twist on the sidewalk stand classic. But you'd probably need to get a liquor license for a neighborhood stand...so this one is better saved for your own personal enjoyment.

MAKES 4–6 DRINKS

½ cup vodka

1 cup bottled lemonade

6–8 cups ice

1–2 (12-ounce) cans lemonade hard seltzer, to taste

1–3 ounces simple syrup, to taste (optional)

✦ Add the vodka, lemonade, and ice to a blender. Blend until smooth.

✦ Add the first can of seltzer. Pulse until combined. Depending on desired consistency, add the second can.

✦ For a sweeter lemonade, add the simple syrup to taste. Pulse.

✦ Serve immediately.

> If you don't have lemonade seltzer on hand, you can absolutely just use lemon seltzer or another lemonade-friendly flavor like strawberry or raspberry.

No Sleep 'til Mango Slushy

Don't sleep on mango! Mango hard seltzer is perfect for blended cocktails. While you can add it to the frozen margarita (page 77) and frozen daiquiri (page 66) recipes for flavor, this vodka version is just as tasty.

MAKES
4–6 DRINKS

6 ounces vodka

2 ounces Cointreau

2 cups frozen mango chunks

1–2 ounces simple syrup, to taste

2–4 cups ice

1 (12-ounce) can mango hard seltzer

✦ Add all the ingredients to a blender. Blend.

✦ Serve immediately.

Adult Orange Julius

You're at your hometown mall. After loitering in the bookstore and the fast-fashion stores, you head to the food court. Where is your clique spending their allowance? The Orange Julius, obviously.

MAKES 4–6 DRINKS

½ cup orange juice

½ cup vodka

1 cup milk

1–2 ounces simple syrup, to taste

½ teaspoon vanilla extract

4–6 cups ice

1 (12-ounce) can orange hard seltzer

✦ Add all the ingredients to a blender. Blend. Serve immediately.

> If you are old enough to drink but too young to have encountered an Orange Julius, just kill me now.

Clawsicles

It's genius. The Claw meets Popsicles in this spiked seltzer pop, a perfect summertime treat. Feel free to change up the fruit and seltzer flavors (try pineapple or mango) for different variations.

MAKES 6 ICE POPS

1 cup mixed berries

1 ounce simple syrup (optional)

1 (12-ounce) can raspberry hard seltzer

✦ Blend the berries and the simple syrup, if using, into a puree.

✦ Spoon about a tablespoon of the puree into six ice pop molds.

✦ Fill the molds with the seltzer, being careful not to overfill. Add the pop sticks (either wooden or plastic, depending on what type of mold you have). Freeze overnight.

✦ Once the ice pops are frozen, run hot water over the molds to release. Enjoy immediately!

Of course, it's not necessary to use White Claw for these "Clawsicles." "Trusicles" or "Bud Light Seltzersicles" just didn't have the same ring to it. Feel free to use any brand here!

Sloshed Strawberry Daiquiri

🍋 🍋 🍋

Strawberry. Raspberry. Pineapple. Mango. Just swap out the strawberry seltzer for a different flavor without any added fruit or syrup. It's that easy!

**MAKES
4–6 DRINKS**

4 ounces white rum

2 ounces lime juice

4–6 cups ice

1–2 ounces simple syrup, to taste

1 (12-ounce) can strawberry hard seltzer

✦ Add all the ingredients except the seltzer to a blender. Blend until smooth.

✦ Add the seltzer and pulse a few times. Serve immediately.

If you end up going with a different flavor, such as mango or pineapple, the flavor will be there, but the color won't. If you're trying to achieve an aesthetic, just add in a handful of whatever color frozen fruit pairs with the seltzer you're using.

the **HARD SELTZER** *cocktail book*

Peak Heat Piña Colada

Everyone likes piña coladas. Getting caught in the rain? Not so much. Enjoy this on a hot summer day.

**MAKES
4–6 DRINKS**

½ cup light rum

¼ cup cream of coconut

2 ounces pineapple juice

1 (12-ounce) can pineapple hard seltzer

4–6 cups ice

✦ Add all the ingredients to a blender. Blend until smooth.

✦ Serve immediately.

No Drama Bahama Mama

Maybe you've had quite the week. Or year. Set your sights on that upcoming vacation, and imagine yourself beachside with this cocktail in hand. You're the Bahama mama now.

MAKES 4–6 DRINKS

3 ounces dark rum

3 ounces coconut rum (such as Malibu)

3 ounces pineapple juice

1 orange, juiced

1 lime, juiced

splash of grenadine

4–6 cups ice

1 (12-ounce) can pineapple hard seltzer, to taste

✦ Add all the ingredients except the seltzer to a blender. Blend until smooth.

✦ Add the seltzer. Pulse until just combined.

✦ Serve immediately.

The 9-to-5 Pain Killer

🍋 🍋 🍋

Long day at work? Email headache? Nothing takes the edge off like a painkiller. Watch your pours, however. If you're too heavy-handed, I can't guarantee you won't have a different kind of headache tomorrow morning.

**MAKES
4–6 DRINKS**

¼ cup dark rum

¼ cup pineapple juice

2 ounces orange juice

2 ounces cream of coconut

4–6 cups ice

1 (12-ounce) can orange or pineapple hard seltzer

ground nutmeg, for garnish

✦ Add all the ingredients to a blender. Blend until smooth.

✦ Garnish with ground nutmeg. Serve immediately.

Fizztastic Frozen Paloma

This tart slushy is a nice break from the sweeter frozen drinks out there. Adjust the simple syrup to your taste. If you're looking for a more classic paloma, an on-the-rocks variation can be found on page 85.

MAKES 4–6 DRINKS

½ cup blanco tequila

1 grapefruit, juiced

1 lime, juiced

1–2 ounces simple syrup, to taste

4–6 cups ice

1 (12-ounce) can grapefruit hard seltzer

✦ Add everything but the seltzer to a blender, and blend until the desired slushy texture is reached.

✦ Add the seltzer and pulse a few times.

✦ Serve immediately.

the **HARD SELTZER** cocktail book

Magic Margarita (Frozen)

The ultimate frozen drink is the margarita. As with the frozen daiquiri recipe on page 66, hard seltzer is the magic ingredient here when it comes to flavors. Just swap out the lime seltzer for your favorite flavor. I suggest mango!

MAKES 4–6 DRINKS

1 lime wedge, for salt rim (optional)

sea salt, for salt rim (optional)

½ cup blanco tequila

2 ounces Cointreau

1 lime, juiced

1–2 ounces simple syrup, to taste

6–8 cups ice

1 (12-ounce) can lime hard seltzer

✦ If desired, rub the lime wedge around the rim of the serving glasses to moisten. Dip each rim in the sea salt to coat.

✦ Add all the ingredients except the seltzer to a blender. Blend until smooth.

✦ Add the seltzer. Pulse a few times until just combined.

✦ Serve in the prepared glasses.

Feelin' Bubbly Aperol Raspberry Float

This combines so many delicious things: Aperol, ice cream, hard seltzer, and even fresh fruit (look, it's healthy!). Great as a dessert cocktail—but honestly, don't be held back by time of day.

MAKES 4 DRINKS

1 cup fresh raspberries

4 ounces Aperol

2 cups vanilla or raspberry ice cream

2 (12-ounce) cans raspberry hard seltzer

✦ Divide the raspberries evenly among four large glasses. Add 1 ounce of Aperol to each glass. Muddle.

✦ Divide the ice cream evenly among the glasses (½ cup each). Top each glass with half a can (6 ounces) of seltzer.

✦ Serve immediately.

CHAPTER THREE

Classy Classics

I'm sure the traditionalists out there will call this section sacrilege, but sometimes we have to mix it up. They're classics for a reason, but surely we can *zhuzh* them up a bit!

Hard seltzer gets a bad rap sometimes, but it shouldn't be left out when it comes to a classy night in. There are so many cocktails out there that benefit from a few bubbles, and hard seltzer is the perfect addition if you want to punch up your favorites. And don't think that hard seltzer can only be mixed with clear liquor. You can still mix it up with the darker rums and whiskeys as long as you have the right flavors in mind.

Millennial Cosmo

We'd have to believe a millennial Carrie Bradshaw couldn't turn down the Claw—it's now a staple at NYC bars and rooftop parties. I couldn't help but wonder: what would the rest of the girls think of this seltzer-y variation?

MAKES 2 DRINKS

2 ounces vodka

2 ounces cranberry juice

1 ounce Cointreau or triple sec

1 (12-ounce) can lime hard seltzer

lime wedges or peel, for garnish (optional)

✦ Fill a cocktail shaker with ice. Add the vodka, cranberry juice, and Cointreau or triple sec to the shaker. Shake until chilled.

✦ Strain into two (ideally chilled) glasses.

✦ Top each glass with half a can (6 ounces) of seltzer. Garnish with the lime wedges or peel.

> If you want to go with the classic martini-shaped glass (aka a cocktail glass), make sure you've got oversized ones on hand. This seltzer variation will not fit in your cute Gatsby-esque coupes.

Poppin' Paloma

If you're running short on ingredients, you can just combine the tequila and the grapefruit seltzer and call it a day. But I recommend including the juices listed here. They make even the lower-shelf tequilas go down so much smoother!

MAKES 2 DRINKS

2 lime wedges, for salt rim and garnish (optional)

sea salt, for salt rim (optional)

4 ounces blanco tequila

4 ounces grapefruit juice

1 ounce lime juice

1 (12-ounce) can grapefruit hard seltzer

rosemary sprigs, for garnish (optional)

✦ If a salt rim is desired, rub a lime wedge around the rims of two glasses to moisten. Dip the rim of each glass in the sea salt.

✦ Fill the two glasses with ice. Add the tequila, grapefruit juice, and lime juice. Stir briefly.

✦ Top each glass with half a can (6 ounces) of seltzer. Garnish with a lime wedge and/or rosemary sprig for added class.

Summer in Moscow Mule

Attention, comrades! Summer in Moscow is here with this spiked seltzer variation on the classic Moscow mule. Ginger beer is an absolute must for this recipe; feel free to add more if desired.

MAKES 4 DRINKS

4 ounces vodka

1 (12-ounce) can lime hard seltzer

1 (12-ounce) bottle ginger beer

fresh mint, for garnish

lime wheels, for garnish

✦ Fill four copper mugs with ice. Add 1 ounce of the vodka to each glass.

✦ Split the seltzer and the ginger beer among the four mugs.

✦ Stir and garnish with the fresh mint and lime wheels.

Midsummer Mojito

I don't always love a lime hard seltzer (sometimes it's just a little boring). The mojito is the perfect way to jazz it up. Fresh mint is a must-have!

MAKES 2 DRINKS

10 mint leaves

1 ounce simple syrup

4 ounces white rum

2 ounces lime juice

1 (12-ounce) can
lime hard seltzer

✦ Split the mint leaves and the simple syrup between two glasses. Muddle.

✦ Split the rum and the lime juice between the glasses. Stir.

✦ Fill the glasses with ice. Top off each with half a can (6 ounces) of seltzer.

Fizzier French 75

Mixing sparkling white wine with hard seltzer doubles the bubbles when compared to the classic French 75. Use wine glasses instead of the traditional champagne flute, because you'll need extra room for all the bubbles in this recipe!

MAKES 2 DRINKS

3 ounces gin

1 ounce lemon juice

1 ounce simple syrup (optional)

4 ounces prosecco or other sparkling white wine

1 (12-ounce) can lemon hard seltzer

lemon twists, for garnish

✦ Fill a cocktail shaker with ice. Add the gin, lemon juice, and simple syrup, if using. Shake until very cold.

✦ Fill two wine glasses with ice. Strain the mixture into the glasses.

✦ Top each glass with 2 ounces of prosecco and half a can (6 ounces) of seltzer. Stir briefly. Garnish each with a lemon twist.

The optional simple syrup is for those who like a little extra sweetness.

Twisted Martini

While James Bond certainly wouldn't order this bastardization of a martini, we had to give this cinematic classic a bubbly twist.

MAKES 2 DRINKS

¼ cup gin

1 ounce dry vermouth

1 can (12-ounce) lemon hard seltzer

lemon twists (optional)

✦ Fill a cocktail shaker with ice, and add the gin and vermouth.

✦ Stir! Don't shake.

✦ Strain into two (ideally chilled) glasses.

✦ Top each glass with half a can (6 ounces) of seltzer. Garnish with a lemon twists.

> The more vermouth you add, the "wetter" a martini gets. If you like your martinis dry, rinse the interior of your glass with the dry vermouth instead of adding it to the shaker with the other ingredients.

Down-and-Dirty Martini

Mixing olive juice and hard seltzer is a delicate balancing act, but it can be done! Although a bit strange at first, it certainly starts to grow on you by the time you've reached the bottom of your glass. Or maybe that's just the alcohol?

MAKES 2 DRINKS

¼ cup gin

1 ounce dry vermouth

1 ounce olive juice (optional)

1 (12-ounce) can lemon hard seltzer

olives, for garnish

✦ Fill a cocktail shaker with ice. Add the gin, vermouth, and olive juice, if using.

✦ Stir! Don't shake.

✦ Strain into two (ideally chilled) glasses.

✦ Top each glass with half a can (6 ounces) of seltzer. Garnish each glass with 1 to 3 olives, to taste.

> James Bond was wrong—you should always stir instead of shake when it comes to martinis. Shaking actually breaks off little pieces of ice that water down your drink.

Classy AF Gin Fizz

Do not be afraid of egg whites! The egg whites make this cocktail classy AF. You will be sure to impress when you shake up these extra-fizzy gin fizzes. I do not recommend skimping on the simple syrup and lemon juice here. All are necessary for a proper fizz; the lemon seltzer just brings it all together.

MAKES 2 DRINKS

¼ cup gin

2 ounces lemon juice

1 ounce simple syrup

2 egg whites

1 (12-ounce) can lemon hard seltzer

lemon wedges or peel, for garnish (optional)

✦ Fill a cocktail shaker with ice. Pour the gin, lemon juice, simple syrup, and egg whites into the shaker. Really shake this one up.

✦ Strain into two tall glasses.

✦ Top each glass with half a can (6 ounces) of seltzer. Garnish with the lemon wedges or peel.

Gimme More Gimlet

A gimlet is simple, classic, and timeless. Lime hard seltzer is required here; using any other flavor would result in an entirely different drink!

MAKES 2 DRINKS

¼ cup gin

1 ounce lime juice

1 ounce simple syrup

1 (12-ounce) can lime hard seltzer

✦ Fill a cocktail shaker with ice. Add the gin, lime juice, and simple syrup. Shake until well chilled.

✦ Strain into two glasses.

✦ Top each glass with half a can (6 ounces) of seltzer.

Claw Collins

There is literally no better cocktail for hard seltzer than the Tom Collins. Just swap out the club soda, and you've got your very own "Claw Collins."

MAKES 2 DRINKS

4 ounces gin

2 ounces lemon juice

1 ounce simple syrup

1 (12-ounce) can lemon hard seltzer

lemon wedges, for garnish (optional)

maraschino cherries, for garnish (optional)

✦ Fill two glasses with ice. Split the gin, lemon juice, and simple syrup between the glasses.

✦ Top each glass with half a can (6 ounces) of seltzer. Stir.

✦ Garnish each glass with a lemon wedge and a maraschino cherry, if desired.

National Treasure Negroni

This recipe is inspired by National Treasure Stanley Tucci. The "Tooch" went viral in the spring of 2020 after releasing a delightful video detailing his extra-boozy Negroni recipe. This adaption has that same spirit (and a lot of spirits). Enjoy carefully, and may the odds be ever in your favor.

MAKES 2 DRINKS

¼ cup gin

2 ounces sweet vermouth

2 ounces Campari

1 (12-ounce) can orange hard seltzer

2 orange slices, for garnish (optional)

✦ Fill a cocktail shaker with ice. Pour the gin, vermouth, and Campari into the shaker. Really shake this one up.

✦ Strain into two ice-filled double old-fashioned glasses.

✦ Top each glass with half a can (6 ounces) of seltzer. Garnish each with an orange slice.

New Old Fashioned

We'll give this iconic *Mad Men* cocktail a modern spin by adding a few ounces of orange hard seltzer into the mix. We know that Don Draper would not be a hard seltzer guy, but with that bone structure we certainly won't hold it against him.

MAKES 1 DRINK

1 sugar cube

1 dash bitters (like Angostura)

1 teaspoon water

1 ounce bourbon

½ (12-ounce) can orange hard seltzer (approximately 6 ounces)

orange peel, for garnish

maraschino cherry, for garnish

✦ Put the sugar cube, dash of bitters, and water in a double old-fashioned glass. Muddle.

✦ Add the bourbon and the seltzer. Stir gently.

✦ Garnish with the orange peel and maraschino cherry.

If you don't have sugar cubes on hand, here's a hint: 1 sugar cube = 1 teaspoon sugar.

Everyday Boulevardier

The *New York Times* recently declared the boulevardier the "perfect" Thanksgiving cocktail, so we had to try a spin on it. You can certainly enjoy this all year round, but it's especially great when you're trying to avoid conversation with awkward cousins and opinionated uncles.

MAKES 2 DRINKS

2 ounces rye or bourbon

1 ounce Campari

1 ounce sweet vermouth

1 (12-ounce) can orange hard seltzer

orange peel, for garnish

✦ Fill a cocktail shaker with ice. Add the rye or bourbon, Campari, and vermouth. Stir.

✦ Fill two glasses with ice. Strain the mixture into the prepared glasses.

✦ Top each glass with half a can (6 ounces) of seltzer. Garnish with orange peel.

Southern Seltzer Mint Julep

What is more refreshing than spiked seltzer on hot and humid Derby Day? Next time you have guests, show them some proper Southern hospitality and mix up this winning combination.

MAKES 2 DRINKS

10 fresh mint leaves, plus 2 mint sprigs, for garnish

1 ounce simple syrup

4 ounces bourbon

1 (12-ounce) can lime hard seltzer

ice, crushed

✦ Rinse and dry the mint. Split the mint between two glasses, reserving the two sprigs for a garnish.

✦ Put ½ ounce of the simple syrup in each glass. Muddle the mint and the syrup.

✦ Split the bourbon and the seltzer between the two glasses.

✦ Top each glass with crushed ice and garnish with a mint sprig.

Summer in the City Manhattan

They say the original Manhattan was made with rye, but obviously we had to make some changes. Orange hard seltzer and bourbon work great here for a nice, sippable whiskey cocktail.

MAKES 2 DRINKS

¼ cup bourbon

1 ounce sweet vermouth

2 dashes bitters (like Angostura)

1 (12-ounce) can orange hard seltzer

maraschino cherries, for garnish

✦ Fill a cocktail shaker with ice. Add the bourbon, vermouth, bitters, and hard seltzer. Mix.

✦ Strain into two glasses. Garnish each with a maraschino cherry.

Snap, Sparkle, Sazerac

Bring a little bit of New Orleans to any party with this twist on one of the city's many iconic cocktails.

MAKES 2 DRINKS

2 sugar cubes

6 dashes bitters (like Peychaud's)

2 teaspoons water

3 ounces rye

1 (12-ounce) can lemon hard seltzer

✦ Chill two double old-fashioned glasses.

✦ In a cocktail shaker, combine the sugar cubes, bitters, and water. Muddle.

✦ Add the rye and seltzer. Stir.

✦ Strain into the chilled glasses.

CHAPTER FOUR

Pregame & Party

While the bubbly concoctions offered in the previous chapters are certainly boozy, they all try to find the balance between buzzed and blackout. In this chapter, I've thrown that out the window. This is the real party.

Ranging from classy to absolutely trashy, this chapter has everything from Holiday Party Punch and Cucumber Lime Coolers to Jell-O shots and jungle juice. Make sure you've got a lot of ice and a large punch bowl on hand.

Enter at your own risk, and be sure to hydrate.

Truly LIIT (Long Island Iced Tea)

I know it. You know it. No explanation necessary. I've scaled it back the tiniest bit to account for average glass sizes, but feel free to increase the liquor amounts as desired. You only live once.

MAKES 2 DRINKS

½ ounce vodka

½ ounce rum

½ ounce tequila

½ ounce gin

2–4 ounces cola, to taste

1 (12-ounce) can black cherry or lemon hard seltzer

lime wedges, for garnish

◆ Fill a cocktail shaker with ice. Add the vodka, rum, tequila, and gin. Shake.

◆ Strain into two glasses filled with ice.

◆ Top each glass with 1–2 ounces of cola and half a can (6 ounces) of seltzer. Garnish each with a lime wedge.

There are few recipes where I recommend black cherry hard seltzer. It's for a good reason: black cherry is an extremely overpowering flavor, and you won't get to taste anything else in your cocktail. But in this case...maybe that's for the best?

Adios Mother Fizzer

The "AMF" is not too different from the Truly LIIT...except this one is blue. Be warned: despite its playful color, this drink is not playing. It is 100 percent booze.

MAKES 2 DRINKS

½ ounce vodka

½ ounce rum

½ ounce tequila

½ ounce gin

1 ounce blue curaçao

1 (12-ounce) can orange hard seltzer

✦ Fill a cocktail shaker with ice, and add all the ingredients but the seltzer. Shake until well chilled.

✦ Strain into two glasses filled with ice. Top each with half a can (6 ounces) of seltzer.

Sparkling Jell-O Shots

No party is complete without Jell-O shots! Make these at least 4 hours ahead so that they are completely set by the time your party is in full swing.

APPROXIMATELY 15 SHOTS

1 (3-ounce) package strawberry Jell-O gelatin

1 cup water, boiling

½ cup lime hard seltzer, chilled

½ cup vodka, chilled

✦ In a large glass measuring cup or mixing bowl, combine the gelatin and the boiling water. Stir until the gelatin is completely dissolved.

✦ Add the seltzer and the vodka. Stir well.

✦ Pour the Jell-O mixture into plastic condiment cups. Cover and allow to set for at least 4 hours in the fridge.

Rum One-Two-Three Punch

✦ ✦ ✦

This party pleaser will pack a punch with not one, not two, but three types of alcohol. Feel free to sub in other citrus or tropical flavors here if you don't have pineapple seltzer handy.

MAKES
4–6 DRINKS

½ cup light rum

½ cup dark rum

¼ cup lime juice

1 cup orange juice

1 ounce grenadine

2 (12-ounce) cans pineapple hard seltzer

ice, as needed

limes, sliced, for garnish

pineapple wedges (roughly ½-inch thick), for garnish

✦ In a punch bowl or large pitcher, combine all the ingredients except the lime slices and pineapple wedges.

✦ Float the lime slices. Garnish glasses with pineapple wedges by cutting a small slit in each wedge and placing it on the rim of the glass.

Lemon Drop It Like It's Hot

A sweetened-up version of the martini, the lemon drop is always a crowd pleaser. Heavy on gin and hard seltzer, it packs a greater punch than you think.

MAKES 2 DRINKS

¼ cup gin

1 ounce simple syrup

1 ounce lemon juice

1 (12-ounce) can lemon hard seltzer

2 lemon wedges, for garnish

sugar rim, for garnish (optional)

✦ Fill a cocktail shaker with ice. Add the gin, simple syrup, and lemon juice. Shake until chilled.

✦ If a sugar rim is desired, rub a lemon wedge around the rims of two over-sized cocktail glasses to moisten. Dip the rims in sugar to coat.

✦ Strain the chilled mixture into the prepared glasses. Top each glass with half a can (6 ounces) of seltzer. Garnish each with a lemon wedge.

Seltz on the Beach

Opt for this cocktail instead of sex on the beach. (I mean, think about it. Sand. Everywhere.) This is a bachelorette party classic when combined with any bridesmaid's best friend: spiked seltzer.

MAKES 4 DRINKS

1 cup vodka

½ cup peach schnapps

1 cup orange juice

1 cup cranberry juice

1 (12-ounce) can grapefruit hard seltzer

orange slices, for garnish

maraschino cherries, for garnish

✦ Combine all the ingredients except the garnishes in a pitcher.

✦ Serve over ice. Garnish each glass with an orange slice and a maraschino cherry.

Mermaid Punch

I can't promise Ariel-quality hair, but I can help you live your best mermaid life with this delicious aquamarine punch. Surely King Trident would disapprove, but what can you do? You wanna be where the people are.

MAKES 6–8 DRINKS

½ cup blue curaçao

1 cup light rum

1 cup pineapple juice

1 (750-milliliter) bottle prosecco or other sparkling white wine

2 (12-ounce) cans pineapple hard seltzer

pineapple wedges (roughly ½-inch thick), for garnish

maraschino cherries, for garnish

✦ Fill a large pitcher or punch bowl with ice. Pour in the curaçao, rum, and pineapple juice.

✦ If making ahead, refrigerate at this stage until ready to serve.

✦ Just before serving, top with the prosecco and the hard seltzer. Garnish individual glasses with pineapple and cherries, if desired. Serve immediately.

> Any tropical-flavor hard seltzer will work here. Pineapple is the most on-theme, but the citrus flavors also work well.

the **HARD SELTZER** *cocktail book*

Apple-Picking Punch

Every time I go apple picking, I end up with approximately 50 apples and a bunch of cider. This is a great way to make a dent in your peck.

MAKES 8–12 DRINKS

CINNAMON SUGAR RIM

½ cup sugar

1 tablespoon ground cinnamon

1 orange slice

PUNCH

1 cup bourbon

½ gallon apple cider or juice, chilled

4 apples, sliced

2 oranges, sliced

6 cinnamon sticks

2 (12-ounce) cans hard seltzer, in a seasonal flavor like Bud Light's Apple Crisp

ice, as needed

✦ To make the cinnamon sugar rim, combine sugar and cinnamon in a small bowl. Rub an orange slice around the rims of 6–8 glasses to moisten. Dip the rims in the cinnamon sugar to coat.

✦ In a large punch bowl, combine all the punch ingredients.

✦ Place the prepared glasses near the punch bowl and allow guests to serve themselves!

I realize not all seasonal seltzers may be available to you, so use your best judgment here. Many cideries have also come out with hard seltzers that would work great!

Holiday Party Punch

Ring in the holidays with this festively themed red sangria. And don't forget, a case of hard seltzer (along with this book) makes a great holiday gift!

MAKES 6–8 DRINKS

1 bottle dry red wine

½ cup brandy or cognac

2–4 ounces simple syrup, to taste

1 green apple, sliced

1 orange, sliced

½ cup fresh cranberries

2 (12-ounce) cans orange, raspberry, or seasonal-flavor hard seltzer

ice, as needed

rosemary sprigs, for garnish

✦ In a large pitcher or punch bowl, combine all the ingredients except the rosemary.

✦ If making ahead, combine all the ingredients except the seltzer, ice, and rosemary. Refrigerate. When ready to serve, add the seltzer and the ice, and stir. Allow guests to serve themselves and garnish with rosemary, if desired.

Lost in the Jungle Juice

No explanation needed. Get a large beverage dispenser (at least 4 gallons) or an empty cooler, and, of course, feel free to improvise. Good luck and Godspeed.

MAKES 30 DRINKS

12 (12-ounce) cans citrus-flavor hard seltzer

1 (750-milliliter) bottle vodka

1 gallon lemonade

½ gallon orange juice

½ gallon fruit punch

3 oranges, sliced

ice, as needed

✦ In a very large bowl, pitcher, or beverage cooler, combine all the ingredients but the ice.

✦ Stir. Fill with ice.

> You can get a pack of just one flavor or a variety pack of citrus flavors. The tropical variety pack would also work well here!

Sweet Tea for a Crowd

This is not your grandma's sweet tea. A little boost from hard seltzer makes this a sparkling and sweet summer treat. Adjust simple syrup to taste; if you're a true Southerner, use the full amount.

MAKES 6–8 DRINKS

12 tea bags black tea

4 cups boiling water

ice, as needed

¾–1 cup simple syrup, to taste

1 cup bourbon

2 (12-ounce) cans lemon hard seltzer

lemon wedges, for garnish

fresh mint, for garnish

✦ Combine the tea bags and boiling water. Allow to steep for 5 minutes. Remove the tea bags.

✦ Fill a pitcher with ice. Pour in the tea.

✦ Add the simple syrup, bourbon, and seltzer. If making ahead, wait to add the seltzer until ready to serve. Stir.

✦ Serve with additional ice and lemon wedges, and garnish with mint.

Cucumber Lime Cooler

Simple and refreshing, this is a great last-minute cocktail for a hot day. Just throw everything in 5 minutes before people show up, and you'll look like you totally have your shit together.

MAKES 6–8 DRINKS

10–15 fresh mint leaves

2–3 ounces simple syrup, to taste

1 cup gin

2 (12-ounce) cans lime hard seltzer

2 cucumbers, sliced

1 lime, sliced

1 lemon, sliced

ice, as needed

✦ Add the mint and the simple syrup to a pitcher. Muddle.

✦ Add the remaining ingredients. Stir.

✦ Serve over additional ice.

Recipe Index

Acknowledgments

Thanks to the entire team at Ulysses Press, who have supported me and all of my craziest ideas for many years. They've seen my highs and my lows (particularly at boozy brunch). Major thanks to Anne Healey, Renee Rutledge, Jake Flaherty, and Production Queen Claire Chun for pulling this together into an actual book.

The fabulous cover of this book was designed by the equally fabulous David Hastings, who I put through the ringer to get this one right.

I have to thank my dear friends who make up the Haus of Eleganza in Brooklyn. They've taught me everything I know about day drinking.

Lastly, I have to thank my dear Michael Calcagno, who enthusiastically drank a lot of seltzer. In cold weather. During a pandemic. Where you ride, I ride.

About the Author

Casie Vogel is a lover of all things carbonated, whether it's a hard seltzer or a Diet Coke. She has experience both hosting and attending many a boozy brunch that has transitioned into an all-night affair, thanks to well-mixed drinks. She lives in Brooklyn.